A WARNING SHOT
INFLUENZA AND THE 2004 FLU VACCINE SHORTAGE

Tim Brookes

American
Public Health
Association

American Public Health Association
800 I Street, NW
Washington, DC 20001–3710
www.apha.org

Photograph Credits: Pages 2, 4, and 6: Images courtesy of the National Museum of Health and Medicine, Armed Forces Institute of Pathology, Washington, D.C.; page 16: Image courtesy of the Public Health Image Library, CDC/Dr. Erskine Palmer; page 40: Image courtesy of the Public Health Image Library, CDC; page 52: Photograph by Mario Villafuerte/Getty Images; page 55: Photograph by Don Emmert/AFP/Getty Images.

Cover photographs courtesy of the Index Stock Imagery. Used with permission.

Georges C. Benjamin, MD, FACP
Executive Director

Printed and bound in the United States of America
Set In: Berkeley and Myriad Type
Interior Design and Typesetting: Tara Kelly
Cover Design: Irma Rodenhuis
Printing and Binding by Science Press, Ephrata, Pennsylvania

ISBN 0-87553-049-4
1M 08/05

Table of Contents

Foreword

"'The sky is falling; the sky is falling,' cried Chicken Little." This line from an early 1930s' children's story tells of Chicken Little who misunderstands the cause of an object that strikes him on his head, and because of his misinterpretation, he and his friends meet a tragic end.

There is a lesson in this fable for public health policy makers who fail to interpret correctly the signs of an impending catastrophic vaccine supply failure.

The conquest of infectious disease through the use of vaccines is one of public health's greatest accomplishments. But like most preventive health measures, vaccines cannot work unless they are available. For years public health experts have warned about the fragility and tenuousness of our nation's vaccine supply and, for years, these concerns have gone essentially unheeded.

A Warning Shot is a story of paradoxes. It is about the failure of government regulatory oversight as well as the heroic efforts of public health officials to respond to the crisis. It is the story of catastrophic production failure at one company and the work of others to fill the void. It is a tale about the failure of national leadership to protect our nation's vaccine supply at a time when many of these same leaders were taking great care to prepare for a potential pandemic influenza.

And underlying the whole story is the need for the United States to begin to think more globally; to work together with other countries in the world to ensure a sufficient, stable vaccine supply worldwide in the event of an unpredicted event.

While the sky has not fallen, it almost did, and we remain unprepared to address it.

Georges C. Benjamin, MD, FACP
Executive Director
American Public Health Association

| The Pandemic of 1918-1919

The influenza pandemic of 1918–1919 killed more people than the Great War—between 20 and 60 million people. The World Health Organization called it "the most deadly disease event in the history of humanity;" more people died of influenza in a single year than in the four years of bubonic plague from 1347 to 1351.

A fifth of the world's population was infected, and a quarter of all Americans. Unlike most forms of flu, which most seriously affect children, the sick, and the elderly, this influenza was deadliest for people ages 20 to 40. An estimated 675,000 Americans died of influenza during the pandemic, ten times as many as in WWI—and of the U.S. soldiers who died in Europe, half of them fell to the influenza virus and not to the enemy. *The Journal of the American Medical Association (JAMA)* noted in its final edition of 1918:

"The year 1918 has gone: a year momentous as the termination of the most cruel war in the annals of the human race; a year which marked, the end at least for a time, of man's destruction of man; unfortunately a year in which developed a most fatal infectious disease causing the death of hundreds of thousands of human beings. Medical science for four and one-half years devoted itself to putting men on the firing line and keeping them there. Now it must turn with its whole might to combating the greatest enemy of all—infectious disease."

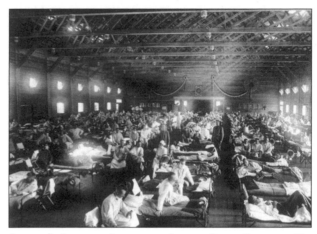

Emergency hospital during influenza epidemic, Camp Funston, Kansas. (*Image courtesy of the National Museum of Health and Medicine, Armed Forces Institute of Pathology, Washington, D.C.*)

The war itself, which involved mass movements of people, often in conditions of lowered immunity, probably contributed to the spread of the disease to North America, Europe, Asia, Africa, Brazil, and the South Pacific. India suffered an especially high mortality rate of roughly 50 deaths from influenza per 1,000 people.

In the long tradition of blaming infectious disease on someone else, the virus was quickly dubbed "Spanish Flu," given that an early outbreak seemed to strike in Spain, where as many as 8 million people may ultimately have died from the disease. Yet in March and April, the first wave of infection had struck the United States as well, arriving by boat, spreading into the heartland, ravaging military camps throughout the country and Kansas in particular. This wave went virtually unacknowledged, perhaps because military camps were notoriously prone to infectious disease.

After a deceptive lull during the summer of 1918, the virus returned to the U.S. in September, apparently making landfall at Boston. The mass movements of people, machinery, and supplies were the perfect vectors for repeated infection and mass transmission, and almost 200,000 Americans died in October alone.

The Armistice ironically made matters worse, bringing together mass celebrations and parades where the virus could spread.

"We had a big celebration downtown," recalled Mary Ferguson Hazlett of Saltsburg, Pennsylvania. "The president of the bank went to Pittsburgh and brought back flags and pom-poms to celebrate in front of town hall.

"The whole town was there, and I think that's when it all started. After the celebration, when the flu started, it went like wild fire. Everyone seemed to get the flu after that. So many people died."

Meanwhile, infected troops began to come back from Europe. Yet even uninfected returning troops added to the public health problem, as the vast numbers stretched the existing hospital staff and facilities beyond the limit. Many fully-trained, able-bodied physicians had been sent to serve with the military, so the sick—many suffering from massive trauma and hitherto unknown ailments such as mustard gas burns—were cared for, to an alarming degree, by medical students. Likewise, nursing staff were so scarce that in some regions of the United States, the Red Cross had to petition businesses to allow volunteer nurses, working evening and night shifts, to be allowed the day off work. Bodies piled up because of the shortage of coffins, undertakers, and gravediggers.

One physician, assigned to Camp Devens near Boston, wrote in late September 1918:

"This epidemic started about four weeks ago, and has developed so rapidly that the camp is demoralized and all ordinary work is held up till it has passed. All assemblages of soldiers taboo.

"These men start with what appears to be an ordinary attack of LaGrippe or Influenza, and when brought to the Hosp. they very rapidly develop the most vicious type of Pneumonia that has ever been seen. Two hours after admission they have the Mahogany spots over the cheek bones, and a few hours later you can begin to see the Cyanosis extending from their ears and spreading all over the face, until it is hard to distinguish the coloured men from the white. It is only a matter of a few hours then until death comes, and it is simply a struggle for air until they suffocate. It is horrible. One can stand it to see one, two or twenty men die, but to see these poor devils dropping like flies sort of gets on your nerves. We have been averaging about 100 deaths per day, and still keeping it up. There is no doubt in my mind that there is a new mixed infection here, but what I don't know....

3

"We have lost an outrageous number of Nurses and Drs., and the little town of Ayer is a sight. It takes Special trains to carry away the dead. For several days there were no coffins and the bodies piled up something fierce, we used to go down to the morgue (which is just back of my ward) and look at the boys laid out in long rows. It beats any sight they ever had in France after a battle."

The effect of the influenza epidemic was so severe that the average life span in the U.S. was depressed by 10 years. Previous influenza epidemics had had a mortality rate of less than 0.1%; the Spanish Flu was so virulent its mortality rate was 2.5%, and the death rate for 15 to 34-year-olds in particular was 20 times higher in 1918 than in previous years.

The virus struck with unheard-of speed. People developed symptoms

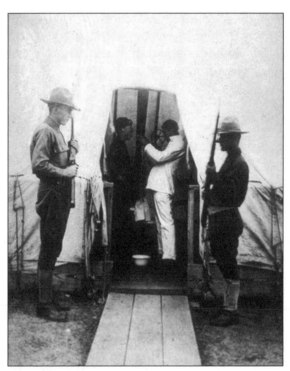

Preventive treatment against influenza, spraying throat. A.R.C. (American Red Cross). Love Field, Texas (*Image courtesy of the National Museum of Health and Medicine, Armed Forces Institute of Pathology, Washington, D.C.*)

on their way to work and died before the day was over. One story told of four women playing bridge together one evening; overnight, three died. Pneumonia was a common complication, and sufferers "died struggling to clear their airways of a blood-tinged froth that sometimes gushed from their nose and mouth." Children made up a skipping rhyme:

> *I had a little bird,*
> *Its name was Enza.*
> *I opened the window,*
> *And in-flu-enza.*

Some thought the epidemic was a form of biological warfare invented by the Germans, or a synergistic product of trench warfare, the use of mustard gases and the "smoke and fumes" of the war—an early parallel to Gulf War Syndrome. A national campaign declared war on the flu, as later campaigns would declare war on cancer and drug abuse, but the metaphor was largely rhetorical: medical science was helpless. It wasn't even clear what was causing the pandemic: it seemed like some kind of influenza, but the responsible agent couldn't be identified, partly because it wasn't yet clear what a virus was, nor how it caused disease. Treatments of all kinds were tried: aspirin, epinephrine, quinine, warm baths, warm drinks, cooling cloths on the head, bed rest, even oil of cinnamon, but the virus resisted them all.

The public health response was at best unhelpful and at worst draconian, issued in the name of science but with very little evidence of effectiveness.

Gauze masks, largely ineffective against an airborne virus such as influenza though perhaps useful in reducing hand-to-mouth transmission, were distributed to healthcare workers and, in an experimental ordinance, to the general population of San Francisco and San Diego, along with the instruction:

> *Obey the laws*
> *And wear the gauze*
> *Protect your jaws*
> *From Septic Paws*

EXCESS MORTALITY in US·CITIES DURING INFLUENZA EPIDEMIC
PERCENT OF POPULATION DYING

CITY	SEPT. 8 -NOV. 23 10 WEEKS	NOV. 24 -FEB. 1 10 WEEKS	FEB.2 - MAR 29 8 WEEKS	TOTAL 28 WEEKS
PHILADELPHIA	.69	.01	.03	.73
FALL RIVER	.59	.05	.04	.68
PITTSBURGH	.59	.12	.06	.77
BALTIMORE	.57	.03	.0	.60
SYRACUSE	.55	.02	.02	.58
NASHVILLE	.55	.16	.12	.83
BOSTON	.50	.12	.0	.62
NEW HAVEN	.49	.13	.0	.61
NEW ORLEANS	.49	.21	.0	.71
ALBANY	.48	.03	.02	.53
BUFFALO	.47	.10	.04	.61
WASHINGTON	.45	.12	.0	.54
LOWELL	.44	.10	.03	.56
SAN FRANCISCO	.42	.31	.02	.74
CAMBRIDGE	.39	.12	.0	.50
NEWARK	.38	.11	.04	.53
PROVIDENCE	.38	.13	.03	.53
RICHMOND	.35	.18	.02	.55
DAYTON	.33	.02	.03	.37
OAKLAND	.33	.22	.01	.56
CHICAGO	.32	.09	.04	.46
NEW YORK	.30	.09	.08	.47
CLEVELAND	.27	.11	.04	.42
LOS ANGELES	.27	.26	.01	.55
MEMPHIS	.25	.02	.09	.37
ROCHESTER	.25	.12	.03	.40
KANSAS CITY	.25	.27	.08	.60
DENVER	.24	.32	.07	.63
CINCINNATI	.22	.13	.11	.46
OMAHA	.22	.20	.0	.43
LOUISVILLE	.19	.04	.14	.37
ST. PAUL	.19	.13	.02	.34
COLUMBUS	.19	.15	.07	.41
PORTLAND	.18	.22	.03	.42
TOLEDO	.17	.02	.0	.17
MINNEAPOLIS	.17	.11	.07	.24
SEATTLE	.16	.18	.02	.36
INDIANAPOLIS	.15	.09	.08	.31
BIRMINGHAM	.15	.15	.0	.29
MILWAUKEE	.15	.18	.03	.37
ST. LOUIS	.12	.18	.04	.34
SPOKANE	.11	.13	.02	.25
ATLANTA	.07	.13	.0	.19
GRAND RAPIDS	.04	.12	.04	.19

Sanitation, Excess Mortality in U.S. Cities During Influenza Epidemic, 1918-19 (*Image courtesy of the National Museum of Health and Medicine, Armed Forces Institute of Pathology, Washington, D.C.*)

The states of Illinois and New York introduced quarantine regulations, and many army camps were quarantined. Saloons, dance halls, and cinemas were closed and public funerals were prohibited as "unnecessary assemblies." Some schools were closed, though not as many or as routine-

6

ly as in Britain or France. Churches were allowed to remain open, but only for minimal services. Street cars—unsanitary, crowded, and poorly ventilated—were seen as especially dangerous. Stores could not hold sales. Some towns required a signed certificate to enter; some railroads would not accept passengers without them. In retrospect, it seems eerily similar to the initial response to SARS in Asia almost 100 years later.

Vaccination was recommended and in some cases administered (the British, for example, used a mixed vaccine against some of the deadlier secondary bacterial infections such as pneumococcus) but as the cause of the influenza was unknown, vaccines were a shot, so to speak, in the dark.

| A Short History of Flu Vaccination

S ince 1919, vaccination has become the most spectacularly successful and cost-effective intervention in the history of medicine.

The earliest vaccines, following Pasteur's experiments, existed outside a public health framework necessary to make them universal and effective, but by the early twentieth century vaccines and the public health infrastructure began to mesh.

The first broad-scale vaccinations were undertaken in armies. During the Boer War at the end of the nineteenth century, during which the first voluntary immunizations took place in the British army, the annual incidence of typhoid and paratyphoid was 105 cases for every 1,000 troops, with a death rate of 14.6 per thousand. A decade and a half later, after the army had officially embraced typhoid immunization (and perhaps other health factors had improved), the incidence of typhoid and paratyphoid was 2.35 per thousand, and the death rate dropped to 0.139 per thousand—about a 100-fold decrease.

Perhaps the best demonstration of the success of a vaccine in the modern age, though, was the astonishingly successful campaign of immunization against diphtheria.

At the turn of the century, diphtheria was one of the main causes of death among children in the developed world, and was not only widespread but agonizingly tragic. It was not unusual for a family to lose two, three or four children to a wave of infection. Affected children would cough more and more weakly as a thick membrane grew in their throats, ultimately closing their airways and suffocating them as parents and the family doctor watched helplessly. It wasn't unusual for grief-stricken parents, having watched their children die, to commit suicide themselves.

Until 1920, Canada suffered some 12,000 cases and 1,000 deaths from diphtheria each year. In the United States, about 150,000 cases and 13,000 deaths were reported annually. After diphtheria immunization was introduced in 1923, with routine immunization becoming more common in the 1930s and 1940s, infection and death rates fell steadily. In 1945 the number of cases in the U.S. had fallen to some 19,000, and as immunization became nearly universal over the next four decades, the victory was almost absolute. By the early Eighties Canada was reporting fewer than five cases a year and no deaths; the U.S. reported numbers in the twenties, almost all among the non-immunized or inadequately immunized individuals. It had become almost impossible to imagine how ghastly the disease had been to families barely half a century earlier.

The History of Vaccination, currently published on the World Health Organization (WHO) web site, lists 13 major diseases for which vaccines have been developed: Smallpox, Rabies, Plague, Diphtheria, Pertussis, Tuberculosis, Tetanus, and Yellow Fever before World War II, and after the war, Polio, Measles, Mumps, Rubella, and Hepatitis B.

Not included on that list is influenza. This isn't because influenza is a rare or minor disease. In an average influenza season, without a major epidemic, flu and its complications cause about 36,000 deaths and 200,000 hospitalizations in the United States, especially among the elderly, the immuno-compromised, and the very young. Influenza vaccine is probably left off the WHO list because it isn't an ideal one-shot-and-you're-safe-for-life vaccine. For several reasons, it is neither universally recommended, nor universally popular.

"Influenza vaccine was first produced in 1945, and has been in use continuously ever since," explained D.A. Henderson, senior advisor at the Center for Biosecurity of the University of Pittsburgh. Henderson is renowned in public health circles as the person who led the eradication of smallpox, and served most recently as Director of the Office of Public Health Preparedness in the U.S. Department of Health and Human Services (DHHS). "It is a vaccine like the other vaccines. In fact, the method for preparation of inactivated polio vaccine follows on from the method used to produce influenza vaccine. Flu vaccine used to be recommended only for those over 65 and others with serious pulmonary or cardiac problems. Some children were given the vaccine, but not many.

"The 1957 pandemic highlighted the potential for influenza to result in fatal pulmonary disease far more frequently than had been supposed and the vaccine began to be more actively promoted. However, the proportion receiving the vaccine in the U.S. was not large," for two reasons. The first was that early flu vaccines produced some very sore arms and systemic reactions, though improvements in its' manufacture largely resolved that problem.

The second was that a new vaccine and a new vaccination is required every year because the predominant circulating strains of influenza virus change frequently, so a yearly vaccination is necessary to obtain reasonably good protection. "Adults are not generally enthusiastic about being vaccinated," Henderson went on. Moreover, "the vaccine often failed to protect as many as 30% or more; and physicians don't do a very good job in promoting preventive measures. Gradually, coverage has become more extensive in the U.S. and, similarly in Europe, although I would guess that European coverage is probably not more than one third to one half what it is in the U.S. Thus, a WHO review of vaccines might overlook influenza vaccine as it is not so often used."

Each vaccine has its own characteristics and problems. Influenza vaccine poses a particular problem because the influenza virus itself is not one stable, predictable pathogen but a constantly moving target.

Influenza is essentially an avian virus. Ducks, for example, may play host to more than a dozen different strains of influenza virus. This doesn't mean they're chronically sick. Influenza A infections in wild birds generally do not cause any symptoms even though all known subtypes of influenza A have been detected among birds. These subtype classifications are based on the combination of 2 surface proteins on the virus, hemagglutinin (H) and neuraminidase (N). Influenza A viruses with H 1–15 and N 1–9 have been found among birds, but only influenza A strains with H 1–3 and

N 1–2 have circulated widely among humans. A virus develops strategies that enable it to survive in a host, sometimes to mutual benefit. Many species, including humans, have substantial numbers of viruses in our bodies at any given time, not doing us any appreciable harm.

But every time a virus reproduces, genetic variations occur. Most of these are harmless, but in the relatively recent past certain specific variations allowed avian influenza viruses to cross from their usual hosts into mammals, especially pigs, horses, and humans.

Influenza viruses change in two ways. One, called antigenic drift, is a gradual, continual change in the virus that occurs as the virus replicates. It is because of the constant nature of this type of change that influenza vaccines are evaluated annually and strains are updated frequently. The other type of change—antigenic shift—is a more drastic change in the influenza virus where the H or N are completely replaced. Viruses can acquire new H/N components from animal reservoirs, and, if easily transmissible from person to person, can cause unforeseen pandemics. **(See sidebar)**

Influenza A Evolution

Year	Influenza Strain	Impact
1874	(H3N8)	
1890	(H2N2)	Pandemic
1902	(H3N2)	
1918	(H1N1)	"Spanish" Flu, pandemic
1933	(H1N1)	First strains isolated
1947	(H1N1)	Variation detected
1957	(H2N2)	"Asian" Flu, pandemic
1968	(H3N2)	"Hong Kong" Flu, pandemic
1976	(H1N1)	"Swine" Flu, non-epidemic
1977	(H1N1)	"Russian" Flu, epidemic
	(H3N2)	
1997	(H5N1)	"Bird" influenza

This constant antigenic change down the years means that every flu season demands new vaccines. For the time being, at least, almost all flu vaccine is produced the way it has been produced for more than half a century: in eggs.

| Making Flu Vaccine

The process by which flu vaccine is made says a great deal about the development of vaccine science, but also about the limitations of egg-based vaccine making, especially in times of crisis and shortage. It also says a great deal about how the necessary infrastructure has grown to coordinate the activities of makers and regulators, public health agencies and commercial operations, activities as local as a chicken farm and as global as the WHO.

Few people are as directly involved in vaccine production as Jim Robinson, Vice-President of Industrial Operations at Aventis Pasteur in Swiftwater, Pennsylvania, a subsidiary of the French pharmaceuticals group Sanofi-Aventis. (Since this interview, Aventis has changed its name to Sanofi Pasteur U.S.) Robinson is in charge of the largest production line of flu vaccine for the U.S. market, a line that can turn out about 50 million doses a year.

The process of making a flu vaccine consists of two converging paths: the selection of the strains to be included, and the manufacturing process itself.

The vaccine is trivalent—that is, it consists of three different virus strains. Each February, WHO doctors meet virologists to identify the three flu strains (two strains of Influenza A, one of Influenza B) they think will

15

be dominant during the following winter.

"What makes flu complicated," Robinson explained, "is that the selection of the strains begins in February and the final selection isn't made until April or so, when the third strain is identified. All of the vaccine doses have

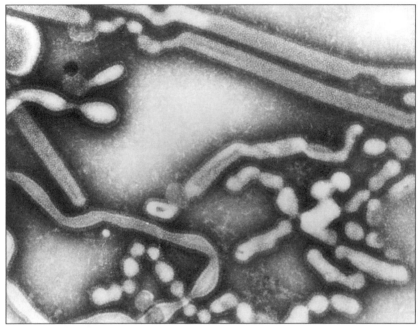

Transmission electron micrograph of influenza A virus, early passage.
(*Image courtesy of the Public Health Image Library, CDC/Dr. Erskine Palmer*)

to be produced—manufactured in eggs, formulated, filled, and packaged— by the end of October, because in general people stop buying vaccine in November. So we have about six months to manufacture. We have only about seventeen weeks to fill and package all of our flu vaccine from the time the last strain is named until the time when our last dose has to be out the door."

Expanding capacity, then, is limited not only by the physical properties of the plant, but also by the small window of time available for production. Flu vaccine makers and the Centers for Disease Control (CDC), Robinson said, have been working to get the message out that the vaccination period doesn't need to end in November, and that useful vaccination can take place in December and even January "and still protect the public from any circulating virus." To the extent that they can extend the immunization season, then, they can also extend the production season and make more doses available.

Aventis also tries to extend the time available for manufacturing at the other end of the process. Making the vaccine actually begins even before the WHO names the first of the three strains in February. In the previous December, a full year ahead of the flu season in question, Aventis makes a best guess at a handful of likely candidates and has some seed virus already in production. "If we wait until February, we have much less capacity. By the time they name the first strain, we're ready to start our second strain."

In December, then, Aventis begins gathering healthy, live chicken eggs.

"We start with an embryonated egg," Robinson said. "They're fertile eggs, and they're incubated at a hatchery for eleven days before delivery."

Aventis has two hatcheries and multiple farms in neighboring states feeding each of those hatcheries, "and we have a very strict biocompliance and biosecurity efforts at all those facilities. Biosecurity not so much to protect them from terrorism, though that's a new thought, for sure, but from microbial contamination—that is, there are always circulating strains of avian influenza that will kill the chickens. We need to protect our flocks from avian influenza, so we have very strict procedures to prevent any bird that might be contaminated from coming into the farms, to protect the farms from any vehicle coming from other farms that might be infected, as well as a battery of testing procedures on the farms to make sure there are no infections. We also have multiple farms, so if one farm should become infected, it doesn't affect our overall supply from other farms."

Before the eggs leave the hatchery, they are inspected to make sure they are fertile and uninfected. "A virus needs a living organism in order to grow, so a dead egg or a non-fertile egg wouldn't help us at all." The egg is inspected by a process called "candling." Once this meant that the egg was simply held up to a candle; now a high-intensity light is shone on the surface of the egg. If the embryo is alive, the light scares it, and it twitches.

"The veins that connect to the embryo run up around the outside of the egg, so you can also see the vein structure. If the fluid around the embryo is transparent, it means the egg is not infected with bacteria. If the egg is infected, the fluid inside the egg appears black or green. So with the light you can check the color of the fluid, but you can also check for a healthy embryo."

This process takes place at the farm, at the hatchery and again during the manufacturing process. At the Aventis plant alone, staff shine lights on and examine more than 100,000 eggs a day, stacks and stacks of rack upon rack of eggs.

It's in examining and simply moving so many eggs around the plant that egg-based vaccine is so much more labor-intensive than cell-based culture, which may one day replace egg-based vaccine production. Cell culture is in most respects parallel to egg-based culture, explained James Matthews, Aventis' Director of External Research and Development. Instead of bringing racks and racks of eggs in through the door, though, the company takes vials of a specific cell line out of a freezer and puts them in biogenerators; and instead of the seed virus being injected into eggs, it is used to infect host cells growing in a hospitable growth medium in a stainless steel tank, somewhere between 500 liters and 10,000 liters in capacity, carefully regulated for pH and oxygen levels. The flu virus mutates so easily and often that a cell line that works well for one strain of virus may not be a good host to another strain, and the company can't afford to have two strains develop well and the third develop poorly. Aventis has set up a partnership with Crucell in the Netherlands to develop cell culture vaccines, Matthews said, but that is in a pre-clinical stage of development and full-scale production, even if everything goes well, is still years away.

After the egg has been inspected at the plant, it is ready to have the "seed" virus added, but that virus has come a long way to reach the plant.

"During the year," Robinson went on, "there is surveillance of strains and outbreaks around the world." During the northern hemisphere's summer it is the southern hemisphere's winter, with its flu season, and the WHO, the CDC, and other agencies constantly monitor and collect strains of virus from human flu sufferers. Historically, the strains found in the two hemispheres were often quite different; in recent years, thanks to the increase in global travel and the spread of flu, the two sets of strains are more likely to have some overlap or even to be identical.

18

Candidate strains are submitted to the U.S. Food and Drug Administration (FDA). "When the FDA finds a candidate seed that they're happy with, they share it with all the manufacturers."

Even that step isn't straightforward, and requires two other acts of tweaking. The dominant strain out in the real world—the "wild" virus"—may not replicate very well or very rapidly in eggs. A relatively new step in the process then removes the RNA of the "wild" virus and inserts it into another, higher-producing flu virus that will produce more virus per egg. The resulting genetic combination has the necessary proteins of the wild virus but helps to accelerate production. (This process may be carried out by government or commercial labs.)

The other important intermediary step involves the fact that the seed virus has been selected because it has been widespread and effective in multiplying in humans—but the very genetic mutations that have made it successful and virulent in humans may mean that it doesn't reproduce very well in chicken eggs: it may have been an avian virus early in its genetic history, but it left home a long time ago. "If you take a human virus and put it in a chicken egg," Robinson continued, "the first time you generally will not get a high-producing virus." While the seed virus is being prepared by the CDC, then, it is passed several times through eggs, so the variants that can adapt well and reproduce rapidly in eggs can be selected, and those that adapt less successfully can be rejected. "You can adapt the virus to the egg itself."

If a variant becomes too potent, though, it will kill the embryo. "The trick is to get as much virus as you can without actually killing the embryo."

At this point in the process, the two paths converge, and the seed virus arrives at the Aventis plant and is injected into the eggs.

The eggs, held upright in trays, pass along a conveyor belt. "A punch comes down and punches a hole in the top of the egg, and then a needle comes down within that punch and inserts a small amount of virus into the allantoic fluid. It doesn't go into the embryo itself, it goes into the fluid around the embryo."

This is a fairly remarkable act of precision engineering. Chicken eggs are, needless to say, all slightly different, yet the punch-needle combination has to be so exact that the needle penetrates below the allantoic sac but not into the chick itself. "So we have a few mechanics here," Robinson added dryly.

Workers carry the trays of eggs into the incubator, where the virus grows over two or three days, then candle them again to check that the embryo is still alive, and that there are no signs of green or black fluid that would denote infection, "because we're incubating them at temperatures that would not only help virus grow, but would also help bacteria." Between 7% and 12% of eggs may be thrown out at this screening alone.

"Then we move all those eggs into a cold room overnight. This kills the embryo, but also all the blood and veinage in the egg settles to the bottom and coagulates into something like a pellet. Because the next day we drain all the fluid out of the egg, and letting it all settle prevents any chicken particulate getting into the vaccine."

That stage is called "harvesting." The technicians remove the allantoic fluid from the egg and pass it through a series of purifications to concentrate it and subsequently filter it through a series of centrifuges and filters.

"We then add the formaldehyde, the material we use to inactivate the virus. Many people believe that you can get flu from a flu vaccine, but we test ours to make sure there is no live virus remaining. None." Other forms of flu vaccine do use live virus. Unlike the inactivated vaccine produced by companies such as Sanofi Pasteur, which is injected into muscle with a needle, the live vaccine is sprayed into the nose. While the common side effects of the injected inactivated virus are a sore arm, and some redness at the injection site, the side effects of the live vaccine may involve a runny nose or sore throat. There is still slightly more concern over the side effects of live virus, which is why MedImmune's nasally-inhaled FluMist is certified for use only by healthy people between the ages of 5 and 49 (this may change in the future after more studies), whereas the inactivated-virus vaccine is approved for anyone over six months old, as long as they don't have certain chronic health conditions.

The vaccine then passes through a purification process called sucrose gradient centrifugation. Putting sucrose into the centrifuge creates layers of different densities, and the flu virus migrates to the central bands, allowing the most and least dense layers to be thrown out. This concentrates the virus about 50–60-fold, reducing the volumes of material that need to be handled during the rest of the process.

Sometimes, depending on the strain, more formaldehyde is needed at this point to inactivate any remaining live virus. Then a detergent kills certain contaminants and splits the virus, breaking open the viral shell and separating out the viral protein, making the virus even less likely to be active. The formaldehyde and detergent are then filtered out, and the resulting fluid, rich in viral fragments, is stored as a bulk concentrate.

Unfortunately, this is not the end of the process. "Even if you have fantastic performance from your first two strains and you have a whole lot of material stockpiled, you can't start formulating the trivalent [final-product] vaccine for some time." The flu vaccine in the factory is still being affected by the behavior of the flu virus out in the world at large.

Two strains may have been made in sufficient quantity, and passed for quality—but until the third strain is named, all the plant can do is wait. Sometimes breaking events elsewhere in the world change the strain: the WHO decides that the real threat is from a different strain, just emerging. Worst of all, the last strain to be named is sometimes a low producer, so the entire process is being held up at the last minute by the reproductive behavior of a single strain.

When the seed virus from the third strain finally arrives and the whole process is repeated, Aventis sends the third-strain product to the FDA for release.

"We need to be able to measure its potency to make sure that the potency is the same for all vaccines that are produced for the U.S. We prepare the reagents for the FDA." The reagents are purified antigen, a specially-made product used to manufacture antiserum used in potency testing. "They take those reagents and inject them into sheep in order to obtain antisera. They bleed those antisera from the sheep, and those antisera are provided to all the manufacturers who are manufacturing products for the U.S. to calibrate their vaccines against."

All this takes time, of course. "Until we get that material back to assess the potency of our third strain, we can't start to formulate trivalent bulk...so this is another of those things where we hurry up and wait."

So the third piece of the trivalent puzzle finally fits into place.

"[So far] we've been collecting two strains; we're now making the third strain. We combine those three products, dilute it with a buffer, and fill it into vials or syringes." At this point, probably some time in September, the vaccine is tested yet again, by both Aventis and the FDA, labeled, packaged, and shipped out the door.

| The First Signs of Trouble

At the beginning of October 2004, the flu news, such as it was, concerned the emerging avian influenza—bird flu, officially named H5N1.

Thailand was stepping up its efforts to eradicate the disease after the death of a nine-year-old girl, the 31st avian flu death of the year. Pundits were warning that the epidemic might turn out to be worse than SARS, that although at the moment it could only be spread to humans by contact with birds, the virus might well mutate, making it able to jump from human to human, and disaster would follow. The Canadian company ID Biomedical announced it had won a large National Institutes of Health (NIH) grant to develop a cell culture-based vaccine for avian flu. Aventis Pasteur, a subsidiary of French pharmaceuticals group Sanofi-Aventis, announced that it had won a contract, said to be worth $13 million, to deliver 2 million doses of vaccines against bird flu to the U.S. government. Yet the WHO warned that pharmaceutical companies were in danger of producing too little vaccine, too late. Two million doses may sound like a large number, but events would very soon show that when it comes to broad immunization, what a small number it really is.

"We understand that companies are driven, at least in part, by market forces," said Dick Thompson, the WHO's press officer, "and that right now, there's not the market to motivate companies. (But) we believe that there could be more intensive efforts, more intensive pandemic preparedness efforts."

In the United States, relatively little attention was being paid to the possibility of a flu pandemic. States had been encouraged to draft pandemic flu plans, but very little funding was made available for the effort. Congress also failed to fully fund the President's influenza vaccine request. Moreover, numerous studies concerning the fragility of the public health infrastructure sat on the shelf. In 2004, the CDC produced its national pandemic flu plan (some years later than various other Western nations), but it didn't address certain central issues. How would a vaccine be developed and distributed at short notice? What would be the federal government's role? How would the supply of that vaccine be safeguarded? What would be done in the way of indemnity and compensation for the pharmaceutical manufacturers? Who would be vaccinated first? Those who studied and advised on vaccines were aware of the importance and urgency of such questions, but neither the government, the medical community, nor the public seemed in a hurry to address them.

Physicians and clinics in the United States were just beginning to put out the word that it was time for members of the public to get their annual flu shots before the season got underway, when on October 5 news of a potential catastrophe came from an utterly unexpected quarter: Great Britain.

At 3:00 a.m., a phone call reached the California headquarters of a pharmaceutical company called the Chiron Corporation. The call was relayed to company officials, and then to the Food and Drug Administration (FDA) in Washington: the UK's Medicines and Healthcare products Regulatory Agency (MHRA), roughly the British equivalent of the FDA, had inspected a manufacturing plant near Liverpool owned by Chiron, and had discovered, not for the first time, the widespread presence of a bacterium known as Serratia marcescens.

Serratia marcescens has a curious history, both miraculous and sinister. In 1263 red blotches appeared on communion bread in a church in Bolsena, Italy. The marks were taken as a manifestation of the blood of Christ, and the "miracle of Bolsena" was subsequently painted into a fresco

24

in the Vatican by Raphael. More than half a millennium later, in 1819, a pharmacist from Padua named Bartolomeo Bizio found similar blood-red discolorations in polenta, and, investigating, found the cause was a bacterium. He named it Serratia in honor of the Italian physicist Serafino Serrati, who invented the steamboat, and added marcescens, or "decaying," because the pigment deteriorated quickly. Because of this and other investigative work, Bizio is considered to be the father of modern bacteriology and bacterial biochemistry.

Until its appearance in the Chiron lab, Serratia marcescens made only one other notable public appearance—as an agent in misguided germ warfare studies carried out by the Navy in 1950. In Operation Sea-Spray, Navy vessels released large amounts of Serratia west of San Francisco, assuming the organism to be benign, to test whether an enemy could effectively release bioweapons offshore. At least one hospital reported an increase in cases of pneumonia, and twenty years later, when the Navy finally disclosed the operation, a San Francisco family sued over a pneumonia death they blamed on Serratia (the courts ruled that the government was immune from such lawsuits).

Operation Sea-Spray may or may not have caused infections from Serratia being inhaled, but the bacterium injected directly into the bloodstream could certainly be deadly. Three meningitis deaths in Contra Costa County, California, in 2001, were blamed on Serratia contamination of drugs legally mixed by a Walnut Creek pharmacy. Serratia can also cause heart-valve infection (endocarditis), pneumonia, and septic shock, any of which could be fatal. A flu vaccine contaminated with the bacterium, moreover, would deliver it with maximum effectiveness to those least able to withstand it: the old, the sick, small children, and people with weakened immune systems. Had the contamination not been detected, a grim irony might have resulted: an epidemic caused by vaccination.

"If you injected it, you'd get bacteremia and sepsis," especially in the people most likely to get the vaccine, said Mary York, a Walnut Creek consultant and former director of microbiology at the University of California, San Francisco (UCSF). "It would be horrible."

Discovering the widespread presence of Serratia in the vaccine pools at Chiron's Liverpool plant after previous warnings that the facility was not

25

being run according to safe and healthy practices, inspectors from the MHRA closed the plant and suspended its license to operate.

The outcome was stark: not only would Chiron be unable to provide the United States with almost half its vaccine orders for the 2004–2005 flu season, but there was no guarantee that Chiron would be back in production by 2005–2006, either.

"There can be no conclusive assurance," Howard Pien, president and CEO of Chiron, testified before Congress in November, "that we will be able to meet expectations of the MHRA, and the FDA by March 2005, which will be the start of full-scale manufacturing season. Moreover, because the regulator's GMP standards are ever rising, we cannot say definitively whether we will be able to meet them in future years."

According to the CDC's figures, the United States needed some 100 million doses of flu vaccine, assuming a normal year for flu and a normal rate of demand. A raft of different agencies, public and private, had contracted with Chiron for some 48 million doses. Half the U.S. flu vaccine production for 2004–2005 had perished.

Even worse, it was impossible to make up the shortfall. With Chiron down, health authorities in the United States were down to only two sources of licensed supply, one of which was already at near-maximum production capacity and the other of which produced, in small quantities, a vaccine authorized only for people between the ages of 5 and 49—a range that excluded those at greatest risk.

With winter coming on and the flu season approaching, there was a very real possibility of catastrophe.

The news was not only unexpected and disturbing, but also confusing: Why was the U.S. flu vaccine being made abroad? How could a foreign regulatory agency shut down our supply of vaccine?

| Vaccines in an Era of Globalization

Pharmaceutical companies are an active part of the global economy, often owned in one country but operating, in manufacture as well as sales, in many others. And because it is such a rapidly-developing industry, it often makes more sense for a large company to buy a smaller company that has developed a new product or a new technology than to invest in untried and experimental ventures at its own facilities.

In the early 21st century, one of these emerging new companies was PowderJect.

"PowderJect is a rapidly growing pharmaceutical company," announced its website, "headquartered in Oxford, UK, with facilities located in Europe and the U.S. With a range of products sold under its Evans Vaccines and SBL Vaccine brands, PowderJect is one of the world's largest vaccines companies. PowderJect's portfolio of products includes vaccines for influenza, yellow fever, travel diarrhea, cholera, tuberculosis, polio, tetanus, and hepatitis B. The company's world-class biologics manufacturing facilities are amongst the largest in Europe, and are approved by both the U.S. and European regulatory authorities."

PowderJect had at least two promising new lines that an established pharmaceutical company might want. "PowderJect's technology focus is on the powder injection of medicines, a field in which it leads the world," the website continued. (This needle-free innovation might also change the entire public perception of vaccination, given that fear of needles—called aichmophobia, belonephobia, or tryanophobia—is a common disorder, recognized in the DSM-IV, that, according to the *Journal of Family Practice* affects at least 10% of the population.) "The company is developing a broad range of vaccines based upon this proprietary delivery technology. PowderJect is also the world leader in the field of DNA vaccines, a revolutionary new method of vaccination that offers the potential to protect against and treat diseases such as hepatitis B and HIV."

PowderJect had made a considerable splash, yet it was facing growing losses because of the high costs of research and development, and it was a prime target for buyout. When Chiron made an offer for PowderJect, it came as no surprise to investment experts in the field.

"It was just a question of time," wrote one investment advisor. "Chiron is the sixth largest vaccine player in the world and a major force in Flu vaccination both in the U.S. and in Europe. It's already the second biggest player in the U.S. and the third biggest in Europe, just above PowderJect. Chiron is also interested in DNA vaccinations—where PowderJect's pipeline excels—another point in its favor.

"That said, PowderJect doesn't seem to be short of suitors and this first bid may well flush out others. Analysts said today that other contenders are rumored to be thinking of a move and big pharma like Aventis, Baxter, Shire Pharmaceuticals, GlaxoSmithKline, and Aventis-Pasteur have all been named. All of them could do with strengthening their vaccine operations —and importantly, have the resources to pull off an offer of this size."

All the same, the column ended with advice for potential investors that would turn out to be prophetic: "A high-risk, speculative buy."

Chiron acquired PowderJect in 2003 for $878 million. Howard Pien, the chief executive of Chiron, said that with two manufacturers having dropped out of the American flu vaccine business, the company saw a need for more vaccines in the United States and a good business opportunity. Chiron announced that it would spend $100 million to expand and upgrade PowderJect's Liverpool plant, and planned to ship more than 50 million doses of flu vaccine to the United States, compared with 26 million in 2002.

Yet there were already signs that the Liverpool plant might have problems—signs that were known to the MHRA and, almost at once, to the FDA.

As early as June 2003, the FDA examined the Liverpool plant, at the time in the process of changing hands from PowderJect to Chiron, and found problems in 20 areas of vaccine manufacture and distribution, including high levels of bacterial contamination. Company documents showed that nearly once a month between March 2001 and July 2002, Serratia had been found in vaccine pools even after the contents had passed through ultrafiltration processes. The team also found poor sanitary practices and, worst of all, a failure on the company's part to remedy its own problems.

The FDA team that conducted the June 2003 inspection recommended that the agency pursue official enforcement action against the Liverpool facility. But their recommendation that the FDA initiate enforcement action was rejected. Instead, the FDA requested only voluntary action by the company, and didn't re-inspect the plant to see if Chiron had complied.

The FDA also declined a Chiron request to meet and discuss the company's response plan, and did not respond to the company's requests for assistance. On June 27, 2003, the plant's manager wrote to the FDA that the company "would like to meet with the agency as soon as possible" to review its response plan. He stated, "At this meeting we would welcome the opportunity to present to the agency our Quality Systems Improvements Program." The FDA replied to Chiron over two months later, on September 3, 2003, saying that the company's letter would be placed in its "permanent file." No mention was made of the meeting request, and according to Chiron officials, no meeting ever occurred. When asked during the November 15 congressional briefing about the failure of FDA to meet with Chiron, FDA officials stated that the agency often declines to meet with companies that have presented adequate plans for addressing inspection problems.

When the FDA requests voluntary remedial action by a manufacturer, the FDA is supposed to send the manufacturer the full inspection report to help the manufacturer understand what corrective actions are needed. In the case of the Chiron facility, the FDA did not send the final inspection

29

report to Chiron until June 2004, a year after the inspection occurred and nine months after it was supposed to have been sent. At this point, manufacture of the 2004 vaccine supply was already well underway.

In August 2004, the same problems resurfaced at the Chiron plant. Chiron notified the FDA that some of the vaccine destined for the United States—perhaps as much as a few million doses—was contaminated. Despite this grim news, the FDA largely monitored the situation at Chiron by making conference calls to the company's officials rather than visiting the plant. It also seems as if the FDA did not contact the MHRA to conduct an inspection on the FDA's behalf.

The MHRA, on the other hand, became both concerned and active. When Chiron reported contamination in August 2004, the British sent a team of regulators to the facility twice (from September 13 to 15 and from September 28 to 30), reviewing the company's records and draft investigation report, convening two high-level committees, and ultimately suspending the facility's license. Ironically, the MHRA was not allowed to inform the FDA of what it was doing because of a law protecting trade secrets.

The news about Chiron aroused a storm of criticism directed at the FDA, which only grew in vigor when Merck & Co., the maker of Vioxx, pulled the popular arthritis drug from the market after a study found it increases the risk of heart attack and stroke—findings that had been suggested in earlier research.

In all fairness, though, the FDA was at least partly the victim of the globalization of the pharmaceutical industry. The same internationalization that had made PowderJect attractive to Chiron showed up the weaknesses and inflexibility of the old-fashioned, traditional notion that a corporation might be "American" or "French," and that such a corporation would be regulated by American or French governmental agencies. The FDA found itself trying to monitor an increasingly far-flung series of operations—at a time when the political climate for hiring government regulators was not a sunny one.

| Warning Signs

The vaccine shortage came as little surprise to anyone who knew much about vaccines. The U.S. Government Accountability Office (GAO) had warned of a flu vaccine shortage in 2002; public health officials had been issuing warnings even before then. Other vaccines have also had problems. According to the National Network for Immunization Information, between November 2000 and May 2003, there were shortages of eight of the eleven vaccines for childhood diseases in the United States, including those for tetanus, diphtheria, whooping cough, measles, mumps, and chicken pox. There also had been flu vaccine shortages or miscues for four consecutive years.

In early 2004, for example, there was a shortage of Prevnar, an expensive pneumococcal vaccine used to prevent pneumonia, meningitis, and middle ear infections in children. Production fell by nearly 50%, according to Dick Raymond, President of the Association of State and Territorial Health Officials (ASTHO), and during the resulting shortage, following CDC guidelines, his home state of Nebraska had to cut vaccination programs from four doses down to two eliminating the final two boosters. But this sent the message that those two boosters weren't really necessary anyway. "Every time this happens it disrupts the schedule and undermines the whole effort to get parents to comply and get their children vaccinated by age two," Raymond said.

Similarly, between 2000 and 2002 a tetanus vaccine shortage meant that a number of states including Nebraska had to stop advising that people routinely get a booster every ten years. "There was still enough to give shots if you stepped on a nail or cut yourself," Raymond went on, "but it really hurts your efforts at educating people how important a routine vaccination schedule is."

Pharmaceutical companies, however, don't tend to see those years as having been years of shortage. Chris Grant, former Vice President for Government Policy at Aventis Pasteur (she has also worked at Merck, and has served as Commissioner for Health and Senior Services for New Jersey), explained some of the complexities that make the system so hard to fix.

"We have a saying: 'If you've seen one flu season, you've seen one flu season.'" Every year is different because of strain selection, the complexities of the manufacturing process, the unpredictable severity of the flu season, and perhaps above all, the vagaries of public demand.

This is perhaps the most intractable issue: the exquisitely sensitive and volatile outlook of the public. Because flu is generally, despite its annual toll of some 35,000 deaths in the U.S. alone, not viewed as a very dangerous disease, and because (therefore) flu vaccination is neither mandatory nor even strongly and universally recommended by practitioners, and perhaps also because widespread vaccination against flu is relatively new, the entire question of whether to get a flu shot is subject to all kinds of fluctuation in individual and collective whim. And whim is sensitive to gossip, rumor, ignorance, and media coverage, all of which tend to swirl and muddy the message from the CDC, the state health department, or the individual practitioner.

This all has a direct effect on the issue of flu vaccine supply. Again, Grant said, there's a saying in the trade: "Demand will drive supply." "If there were a predictable increasing demand for vaccine, the manufacturers can plan to increase overall capacity to shoot for an ever higher target." Today only 70–80 million Americans get flu shots, even though immunization is recommended for roughly 185 million.

Even though demand has increased—from some 40 million doses in the early Nineties—demand is neither predictable nor bound to increase in any given year. In fact, there even seems to be the worst possible situation—an out-of-phase wave effect. Demand shunts up and down, supply tries to anticipate the level of demand, like a rock-paper-scissors player, and as a result it sometimes seems to manufacturers, Grant said, as if the two are constantly out of sync, with the makers producing less when more is demanded and more when less is demanded.

Here's another layer of difficulty: with two major players supplying most of the U.S. flu vaccine market, each is left second-guessing not only the public but the other manufacturer. "The market is competitive, so we don't know what the other guy plans to produce in any given year," Grant said.

She gave two examples that show how easily and dramatically the supply-demand equation can get pulled out of shape.

One has to do with the complex and powerful little whirlwinds produced by the combination of media coverage and public reaction. During one recent flu season, she said, a season that had started off slow and mild, the news broke after Thanksgiving that several children had died of flu in Colorado. These sad events exploded in the media, and as a result the rate of late-season vaccinations among children rose sharply. At once, individual areas in the U.S. began reporting shortages of vaccine, raising public alarm still farther.

Yet subsequent study by the CDC revealed that the pediatric flu season had in general been unexceptional—it hadn't been an unusually dangerous flu for children after all, despite this flurry of alarm. The following year, though, demand for vaccinations among 6–23 month-old children soared from 7% to 57%.

Grant's other example showed how dramatically the supply-demand equation can be distorted by the manufacturer. In 2004, she said, "I was surprised to hear—surprised, knowing that '03 hadn't been a terribly strong season—that Chiron out of the blue had dramatically raised its projections up to 50 million doses to be imported into the U.S." This not only added tens of millions of doses to its own output, but would have pushed the overall U.S. supply to the 100-million-dose mark.

From an economic point of view, this was not only risky but even bizarre. Yes, Chiron had recently bought PowderJect and was planning to renovate and expand the Liverpool plant so it could raise the company's production capacity, but the American public had never bought 100 million doses in a year.

"The market had never absorbed anything like that number," Grant said. The usual figure hovered around 70 million, and even in a year when 80 million were sold and bought, quite likely several million would go unused.

The net effect of this curious strategy was that when Chiron ran into trouble, the extent of the damage to the nation's supply was exaggerated: instead of the U.S. losing some 20–25 million doses, it looked as if its supply was being cut by half.

"The media became fixated: it was supposed to be a hundred-million-dose year," Grant said. But this was a mirage. "Nobody knew if a hundred million doses had even been *ordered*."

It's hardly surprising, then, that pharmaceutical companies have long been migrating away from developing, manufacturing, and selling vaccines. Even as the number of vaccines has risen since the 1970s, the number of companies in the U.S. making vaccines has fallen, from 25 down to the single digits. By 2004, the number of U.S. companies making injectable flu vaccine was two: Chiron, an American company making vaccines abroad, and Aventis Pasteur, a subsidiary of a French company making vaccines in the U.S.

Why don't more major American drug companies make flu vaccine? In addition to Grant's reasons, it's because flu vaccine just isn't a very attractive business venture, especially in an industry accustomed to double-digit annual growth.

First, the vaccine market in general isn't very big. The global vaccine market is about $6 billion a year; the global market for drugs in general is about $340 billion a year. Vaccination is such a cost-effective intervention that there just isn't much money to be made from it. A single childhood vaccination may prevent a disease for life; by contrast, someone taking a statin medication for heart problems may easily take thousands of pills over the course of a lifetime. In 2003, total global sales for Merck's seven vaccines were $1.056 billion, according to Merck Vaccine spokeswoman Christine Fanelle. By comparison,

Singulair, its respiratory product, brought in $2 billion alone, and Fosamax, its osteoporosis medicine, grossed $2.6 billion. With an annual flu shot costing some $8–$10, the profit margin, by the standards of the pharmaceutical industry, is relatively thin.

Second, the flu vaccine market is especially unpredictable and costly. Flu viruses mutate easily, so each year's vaccine needs to be based on a different combination of variants that seem likely to be the dominant strains during the coming season. Instead of being able to create a vaccine and then putting it into production, watching it become steadily more profitable each year as more units sell, the maker has to reinvest time and money each season.

Third, because a different vaccine combination is made up for most seasons, and because the shelf life of the vaccine is only one year, any doses that aren't sold one year are useless the next, so they end up being destroyed.

Fourth, making flu vaccine under stringent contamination-free conditions is extraordinarily labor-intensive. As described earlier, flu vaccine is made by injecting virus into fertilized chicken eggs. Each egg must be hand-inspected and hand-injected, and even then it produces only four or five doses of vaccine. This means that it's almost impossible for a plant to crank up production at short notice—as the U.S. discovered to its cost in late 2004.

Fifth, this labor-intensive process creates yet another disincentive for large drug companies to move into the flu vaccine business. At some point in the near future, flu vaccines will be grown in cell cultures rather than eggs, a potentially much easier and cheaper process. So what is the incentive for anyone to invest millions of dollars in egg-based production now, when that process will likely be obsolete?

Sixth, working with biologically active vaccines is much more delicate and potentially volatile than working with ordinary prescription drugs, which means that it is not only expensive and time-consuming, but it requires rigorous quality control and oversight. As the Chiron episode demonstrated, without adequate oversight the potential for disaster is terrifying. For several major companies, though, such oversight has cut into their profits to the point where they would rather simply quit the business.

The Warner Lambert factory in Rochester, Michigan, for example, made a flu vaccine called Fluogen for at least twenty years, but had increasing problems complying with government regulations that were introduced in the 1990s in the aftermath of the contamination of blood products by the AIDS virus and other catastrophes. In 1998, Warner Lambert quit the business and sold the factory to King Pharmaceuticals. But the FDA continued to find violations, including some considered so serious that it shut down the plant twice in 2000. After the second time, King said it would stop making Fluogen rather than commit more money to trying to bring the plant into compliance.

But Dr. Jesse Goodman of the FDA defended its policies, saying that they were the "gold standard" for safety worldwide. If companies could not measure up or chose not to, he said, it might be better for them to pull out.

Unfortunately, this leads to a seventh reason why the U.S. flu vaccine supply was so easily compromised: when Chiron was closed down, most European countries that had contracts with Chiron could simply order the shortfall from one of nearly ten other manufacturers.

In England, for example, the National Health Service bought the 14 million doses of flu vaccine that it needed from five or six suppliers, said Alison Langley, a spokeswoman for the Department of Health. Two million of those doses were to have come from the Chiron factory in Liverpool. "But we were able to make that up with additional purchases from elsewhere," Ms. Langley said.

However, American healthcare officials couldn't make up the shortfall with additional purchases from elsewhere because other manufacturing plants didn't meet FDA standards, or hadn't been inspected to see if they did meet those standards. This doesn't mean that these plants, operated by major international pharmaceutical companies, were substandard and prone to turning out infected batches of vaccine. The problem was that the FDA and the regulatory agencies from other developed nations were working from different sets of guidelines, and no universally acceptable set of standards had been worked out. The outcome was horribly ironic: the FDA's "gold standard" failed at the Chiron plant, one of the few that had been inspected and passed for sale and distribution to the U.S., yet at the same time it prevented U.S. agencies from buying from other plants that were likely turning out perfectly good vaccine.

Most of these difficulties applied to drug makers everywhere, yet these manufacturers weren't abandoning the vaccine business as rapidly as they were in America. Production, then, was not as big an issue as supply. The FDA had unintentionally narrowed the range of supply to the point where it was easily choked. But there was one more major difference between the U.S. and other countries when it came to acquiring vaccines in general, and the influenza vaccine in particular. That difference was how vaccine was bought.

Most countries buy vaccines, including flu vaccine, centrally and in quantity. Each province in Canada, for example, calculates how many doses will be needed for the coming flu season, and orders that number, sometimes buying in consortium with other provinces to take advantage of the economies of scale. Immunization is seen as being a sufficiently high priority that public health funds are made available for these large buys.

"We're a bit more structured than the U.S.," said Dr. Michael Finkelstein, Associate Medical Officer of Health Communicable Disease Control at Toronto Public Health. His agency, unlike some municipal health agencies in the U.S., doesn't purchase vaccine—it orders it through the province, which provides the requested number of doses at no charge to the local health agency.

"Since 2000, anyone in Ontario can get a flu shot at no charge to the patient or the physician." Other provinces offer flu shots free of charge to high-risk patients: the elderly, the young, and people with chronic illness such as diabetes, cancer or heart disease.

To safeguard this supply, Canada has decided to invest in a pandemic supply contract. "We realized a number of years ago that we needed to make sure of our long-term supply." A consortium of provinces and territories placed a long-term bulk order with ID Biomedical, Canada's only domestic flu vaccine producer, and supplemented that order with another large order placed with Aventis. When the Chiron crisis arose, the main difficulty facing Canadian health officials was not from their own residents but from Americans coming across the border looking for flu shots.

The United States buys some vaccines in bulk, but flu vaccine is different. A myriad of different organizations and agencies order small quantities from a distributor or directly from the manufacturer. Perhaps as much as nine-tenths of all flu vaccine reaches its destination through a fragmented and fiscally inefficient patchwork of private providers—an arrangement that isn't centrally controlled or coordinated, either. Not only did this mean that Americans were paying more for their flu shots, it meant that when a shortage arose, the entire provider system would collapse.

Not only would the U.S. flu vaccine supply be cut by half, but its ability to deliver what vaccine was still available would be cut by 90%.

| The First Days of the Shortage

On October 5, when the Chiron news broke, Chris Grant was on Capitol Hill. "We were literally standing in line to go into a hearing at which Julie Gerberding [the CDC director] was testifying at the request of Rep. Weldon of Florida." It was a sign, she said, of how poorly Congress understands the complexities of the vaccine system. Weldon wanted to forbid the CDC to spend money on any vaccine that contained preservatives. Gerberding was trying to explain that there was no evidence that linked preservatives in vaccine and any resulting illness, and in any case it was impossible to try to change the entire nation's vaccine production overnight, when according to Grant, "Dr. Gerberding was monitoring her Blackberry for the news about Chiron. She broke off her own testimony and said, 'I'm sorry, we have a bigger issue here.'" The preservative question seemed suddenly very small.

At the same moment Dick Raymond was, by an ironic coincidence, in Washington, D.C., on behalf of the National Vaccine Advisory Committee (NVAC), meeting with representatives of the CDC and the other major players in the vaccine world, discussing how to improve vaccine supply and how to increase the number of people who get flu vaccine.

As soon as the news was announced, the agenda went through a phase shift. Several members of the NVAC were also members of the Advisory

This photograph was taken during a 2004 CDC Press Conference, and included Director of the CDC, Julie Gerberding, M.D., M.P.H., standing at left, and virologist Dr. Nancy Cox, Chief of the Influenza Branch in the National Center for Infectious Diseases (NCID), speaking at the podium. (*Image courtesy of the Public Health Image Library, CDC*)

Committee for Immunization Practices (ACIP), and they broke off the meeting, retreated to hold a conference call with the other ACIP members, and in a dramatic example of real-time public health, came up there and then with the recommendations that the CDC restrict vaccine to eight high-risk groups.

The meeting continued without them, but many members were distracted because of cell phones and Blackberry messages as groups back home struggled to work out how to respond to the news.

"It was kind of neat to be in the middle of it all," Raymond said. By the end of the day he was able to call back to Nebraska and let the local officials know what strategies had been drawn up around him during the day.

The following day he called again and ordered an immediate inventory of every public and private healthcare provider in the state to determine who had ordered from Chiron and who from Aventis, who had vaccine in

40

hand or on the way, and who didn't. That evening he was sitting in an airport lounge in Washington, D.C., on a conference call with eight Nebraska health officials trying to decide how to reallocate the available vaccine, and how to get the word out to the public that the vaccine shortage was an inconvenience, but not a catastrophe.

Then he was talking to his staff and saying, "Your regular job's ended or on the back burner for the next three months," and reassigning them to work on the flu vaccine shortage. Raymond shrugged off this massive course correction. "Public health is all about reprioritizing on the spur of the moment anyway."

| Rationing and Redistribution

Following the recommendations of the teleconferencing ACIP, the CDC proposed a soon-to-be-familiar set of guidelines for those at highest risk, who should be the first and potentially the only people to get flu shots:

- All children aged 6 to 23 months old
- Adults aged 65 years and older
- Persons aged 2 to 64 years with underlying chronic medical conditions
- All women who will be pregnant during the influenza season
- Residents of nursing homes and long-term care facilities
- Children 6 months to 18 years of age on chronic aspirin therapy
- Health care workers with direct patient care
- Out-of-home caregivers and household contacts of children less than 6 months of age.

At once, this message, like any ripple in routine, caused problems. Until October 5, said Pat Libbey, Executive Director of the National Association of County and City Health Officials (NACCHO), the message to the public had been "Everyone should get a shot." The abrupt shift of message left people doubting that creed: maybe a shot wasn't so important after all. The news media found a physician in New York City who questioned how necessary flu shots were in the first place. Some over the age of 65 publicly volunteered to give up their shot so someone else could have it—a noble gesture, but a mixed message.

Libbey also felt that one of the core initial decisions was a mistake. "The first day this broke we urged the CDC to further prioritize among the high-priority groups." The point, he said, was another issue of numbers: in many areas of the country there wasn't enough vaccine to cover all the high-risk groups, leaving local authorities to interpret the rules as best they could. "It wasn't done uniformly."

The problem facing American health officials in the days immediately following October 5 was that nobody knew how much vaccine was in the country, nor where it was, nor how to redirect it to those who needed it most. The issue, Libbey said, was "Not only a shortage, but an extraordinary maldistribution, combined with a complete lack of any kind of system or ability to identify where the vaccine actually was. There is no means of tracking the private and public vaccine at any point in time."

Flu vaccine is distributed according to the way it is used. Instead of one customer's entire order going out at once, Grant explained, everyone who has ordered vaccine starts receiving "a proportional share" of their order in late August and early September, so the vaccination season can begin ahead of the flu season. As the fall progresses, each customer receives further doses of vaccine at a rate that more or less keeps pace with the demand for vaccinations. By the time the Chiron news broke, then, thousands of Aventis customers had already received shipments of vaccines, "and much of it was already in the arms of patients."

But how much of the coming season's vaccine had already been shipped (later estimates put the figure at some 33 million doses), and where had it gone? The drug companies' shipping manifestoes were of little use, as they often simply recorded that the shipment had been sent to a distributor or resale merchant. Besides, the makers were private corporations, unaccustomed to turning their documents over to public scrutiny.

Over the next six weeks, an extraordinary effort of cooperation took place, almost entirely behind the scenes. Because some 90% of all flu vaccine is administered by private practitioners, the CDC had no master list of all the physicians, clinics, and nursing homes in the country and no means to get a series of questions and requests out to them so that a master list of high-risk patients could be drawn up. It was largely up to the state and local health departments to do this. An emerging technique in public health informatics was being tested on the run—and all this occurred even while the states themselves were under tremendous pressure, Grant said, and many a governor was saying or thinking "I want answers, I want them now, and I want vaccine in my state."

Likewise, the vaccine makers and distributors were in a new and potentially difficult position as private corporations needed to change their routines in the name of the public good. Information about orders and customers, usually a well-kept secret, were passed to the CDC, and Aventis employees worked sixteen-hour days with federal and state officials to help match the remaining doses with the practitioners who needed them most. Meanwhile, the customers themselves, who had ordered vaccine and in an increasing number of cases had patients knocking on their doors asking for it, had to be persuaded to wait and trust that no deals were being worked out behind their backs, no widespread price-gouging was being planned, and there was no massive government intervention that would leave private providers (and their patients) out in the cold. The opportunities for gossip and paranoia were boundless.

"It was a tremendous and complex collaboration," Grant said, "and it was all based on the willingness of customers who had ordered vaccine to hold and wait and see—to be very patient as these plans were starting to develop at the CDC."

The state of Vermont, for example, immediately canceled state employee flu shot clinics, began an inventory to find out how many doses of vaccine were actually available in the state, and began holding emergency meetings with health care providers, hospitals, home health agencies, nursing homes, and others to discuss options for redistributing vaccine to make sure that it got to those who most needed it.

The inventory came up with some 36,000 doses, of a total of perhaps 86,000 needed to vaccinate all those in the high-risk categories.

In October, the Vermont state health department sent its newly revised Recommendations for Pediatric Use of Influenza Vaccine—October 14, 2004, to pediatric and family health care providers around the state.

Physicians were told to give flu shots only to children age 6 months to 18 years old who had one or more chronic medical conditions that required frequent or ongoing medical treatment, including children on daily aspirin therapy and children with moderate to severe asthma. Beyond that, they should establish a waiting list of all other children age 6 to 23 months, who would be vaccinated should additional vaccine become available.

In an emergency health order dated October 20, the health department essentially froze all vaccinations in the state, forbidding any healthcare agency, private or public, from vaccinating anyone who did not fall within the CDC guidelines. Given that the physicians themselves would be the ones to both monitor and enforce the order, but also the ones in a position to break it, it was in essence a good-faith regulation.

The state also directed health care providers and organizations that had privately purchased vaccine to return a portion of their supply to the Health Department for redistribution—a directive that recovered more than 10,000 doses.

Vermont's Health Department broke down the need: for children age 6 months to 18 years old with serious medical conditions, roughly 7,000 doses of vaccine provided by the Health Department, through its Vaccines for Children program. For nursing home residents, 3,000 doses recovered as a result of the health order or provided by hospitals and a private corporation. For patients in dialysis units, pulmonary clinics, hematology and oncology clinics, infectious disease clinics, and people in specialty care for HIV/AIDS—about 1,000 doses. Another 3,500 doses for certain health care workers who provide direct patient care. For elders in assisted living, adult day care or those homebound, 6,000 doses of vaccine from the Visiting Nurses Association (VNA) of America.

The VNA had donated some 11,000 doses, in fact. This was just one of a series of urgent acts of brokering that were taking place all over the country, as cities and states scrambled to find agencies that had more vaccine than they needed. Generosity, arm-twisting, begging, scrounging—the phone lines of America were hot with the efforts of trying to devise an equitable vaccination system under crisis conditions.

| The Politics of Flu Vaccine

With a fiercely contested presidential election little more than a month away, it was perhaps inevitable that the vaccine crisis should be used as a political weapon. John Kerry claimed that the crisis was an example of mismanagement by the Bush administration.

A few days after the Chiron news broke, during a visit to the nursing school at Lorain County Community College in Ohio, Kerry said, "If you can't plan to have enough of that vaccine, what are they doing with respect to other things that could potentially hurt America in terms of bioterrorism, chemical terrorism, other kinds of things?"

Steve Schmidt, a spokesman for President Bush's campaign, called Mr. Kerry's comments "baseless and hypocritical."

"So few companies make flu vaccines because of a broken medical malpractice liability system that Kerry falsely claims to want to fix but has voted ten times against reforming," Mr. Schmidt said.

The notion that flu vaccine was in short supply because of malpractice litigation is a myth (as we'll see shortly), but Schmidt's misleading attempt at a counterattack was perhaps a hint of retaliation to come.

Almost at once, the e-mail equivalent of a right-wing attack ad began moving through the vast, ethereal circulation system of the Internet, being passed on in whole or in the gist by various individuals and media outlets.

47

After summarizing how the Chiron contamination had caused the flu vaccine shortage (inaccurately referring to Chiron as a British company, an important misstatement), the email moved on to the question "Why is our vaccine made in the UK and not the U.S.?"

It answered its own question in this way:

"The major pharmaceutical companies in the U.S. provided almost 90% of the nation's flu vaccine at one time. They did this despite a very low profit margin for the product. Basically, they were doing us a favor. In the late 1980s, a man from North Carolina who had received the vaccine got the flu. The strain he caught was one of the strains in that year's vaccine made by a U.S. company. What did he do? He sued and he won. He was awarded almost $5 million! After that case was appealed and the appeal was lost, most U.S. pharmaceutical companies stopped making the vaccine. The liability outweighed the profit margin. Since UK and Canadian laws prohibit such frivolous lawsuits, UK and Canadian companies began selling the vaccine in the U.S.

"By the way...the lawyer that represented the man in the flu shot lawsuit was a young ambulance chaser by the name of John Edwards."

In other words, Senator John Edwards of North Carolina, the Democratic Vice-Presidential candidate.

Snopes.com, a web site that collects and evaluates urban legends, declared the story false, pointing out three major flaws.

First, it pointed out, Chiron is an American company.

Second, it went on, American manufacturers did not stop producing flu vaccine when liability lawsuits made that market financially untenable for them. Litigation against vaccine manufacturers did create some problems prior to the mid-1980s, but in 1986, Congress addressed the problem of lawsuits (which were largely over the diphtheria, tetanus, and pertussis (DTP) vaccines, not flu vaccines) with a law establishing the National Vaccine Injury Compensation Program, a no-fault compensation alternative to suing vaccine manufacturers and providers for people injured or killed by vaccines.

Third, "As for the claim that John Edwards secured a $5 million judgment against a U.S. pharmaceutical company on a flu vaccine case, while it is true he had a highly successful legal career representing individuals who had been badly harmed by malfunctioning products or the mistakes of doctors and hospitals (with some sources claiming he won up to $175 million for his clients over 12 years), no flu vaccine lawsuit appears on the list of major cases he has handled....*The Charlotte News & Observer* also was unable to turn up any incidence of John Edwards' handling a lawsuit related to flu vaccine... [and] no record exists of any lawsuit involving Edwards against a vaccine maker."

According to snopes.com, flu vaccines have actually been relatively free of litigation. "According to research by the Association of Trial Lawyers of America, since 1980, there have been just seven cases involving the standard flu vaccine reported in state and federal appellate courts. In five of those cases, the defendant prevailed; the results of the other two are unknown. Seven cases in 24 years does not make a liability crisis.

"Additionally, the role that lawsuits have played in the flu vaccine market is minimal. From 1990 to 1995, there were two lawsuits filed per 10 million doses of vaccine, according to the U.S. Department of Health and Human Services."

There were many problems facing the U.S. flu vaccine supply, but lawsuits were not among them.

| Scrambling

By mid-October the *Boston Globe* was reporting a "feverish" dash for flu shots among the elderly and chronically ill, with people as old as 94 waiting in line for three hours. Lines as long as nine hours were reported in California. One woman died after hitting her head when she passed out or fell while waiting.

The New Jersey town of Bloomfield, population 70,000, finding itself with only 300 remaining doses of flu vaccines set up a lottery among the elderly, adults with chronic illnesses, pregnant women, nursing home residents, and health workers. At the time, the lottery process struck some as alarming, even callous. Within a month, however, other municipalities all over the country had followed Bloomfield's example.

With vaccine in such short supply, and with the public so alarmed, conditions were perfect for profiteering, fraud, and theft.

Pharmacists at several Massachusetts hospitals said that suppliers had offered to sell them shots in recent days for as much as $90 a dose, more than ten times the normal price. More than half of pharmacists surveyed across the nation reported that they had been contacted by vendors selling vaccine at drastically inflated prices. Bob Moura, director of pharmacy services at Quincy Medical Center, said he received such an offer from a company in Fort Lauderdale, with a quote for a 10-shot vial of the vaccine:

Senior citizens wait in line for their flu shots at the Albertson's Super Market October 12, 2004, in Bossier City, Louisiana. About 100 elderly waited in line two hours for a limited supply of flu vaccine. (*Photograph by Mario Villafuerte/Getty Images*)

$900. The customary price before the Chiron episode: $68.

Francois Bourdeau, director of marketing for an e-mail security company, said that spammers and con artists were taking advantage of the shortage by offering the vaccines through e-mails and on web sites using a variety of methods, such as pinging and hijacking servers, to profile and target people most susceptible to the scams. His company, he said, estimated that about one in 20,000 people targeted by spammers falls for the schemes. Since the flu scams may number in the "high millions," according to Bourdeau, a significant number of people might have already responded to the scams, which were charging as much as $600 for a single shot.

"Sixty percent will be downright frauds, where the only goal was to get people's credit card information," Bourdeau said. The other 40 percent, according to Bourdeau, led to web sites that might actually offer something—possibly the real flu vaccine, possibly some other substance. "You can end up with pretty nasty stuff," he said.

Attorneys-general in Kansas, Texas, Connecticut, and Florida filed suit against Meds-Stat of Florida for inflating the price of flu vaccine by 900%. Meds-Stat was ordered to turn its inventory of vaccine over to the Florida Department of Health for free distribution to the public. ASAP Meds of Fort Lauderdale was also sued for alleged "unfair and deceptive trade practices regarding the pricing of pharmaceuticals."

Thefts were reported from clinics and doctors' offices in Miami, Pennsylvania, and Colorado.

Apart from more obvious unethical activities, the entire question of allocation of flu shots raised major ethical problems of its own: Who should get the available shots? Who should decide? Who should oversee the process? Who should enforce it?

The target populations for flu vaccination, as described by the CDC guidelines, include people older than 65, children 6 months to 23 months in age, people ages 2 to 64 with chronic illnesses, medical workers directly involved in patient care, and several smaller "risk groups."

The problem was, at that moment there were simply nowhere near enough shots to cover those populations.

In an op-ed commentary published on November 2, Dr. Arthur Caplan, Director of the Center for Bioethics at the University of Pennsylvania, wrote:

"John Stuart Katz is at high risk of dying if he gets the flu.... When I spoke with him recently, Katz wanted to know if I had any 'connections' to help him get a flu shot. Five years ago he underwent a kidney transplant using an organ donated by his wife. At 66, Katz takes medicine that helps his transplanted kidney keep working, but which also weakens his immune system. As a professor, he is constantly exposed to coughing and sneezing in classrooms. But his doctor has no flu vaccine and Katz is afraid he might die if he catches the flu. And he should be worried since he's in a very high-risk category.

"I told him I did not have any connections but I would see what I could do. What I did not tell him was that at least four doctors have asked me if I wanted to get a flu shot even though I am not in any of the high-risk categories. I told them no. And if you are not over the age of 65, under the age of 2, pregnant, living in a nursing home, someone who works with patients in hospitals or nursing homes, or someone with an immune disorder —the people at the greatest risk of dying from the flu —you should say no to a flu shot, too."

Caplan summed up some of the ethical inconsistencies of the vaccine shortage: at Louisiana State University, he said, any student who wants a flu shot is apparently getting one. Students receiving shots at the student health center are not being screened to be sure that they're in one of the high-risk categories.

"Some doctors are vaccinating their families, friends and long-time patients, even if they're not in high-risk categories.... Some chain stores where many people go to get their annual flu shots are giving them out no questions asked."

Not just chain stores and student health centers, but the U.S. Congress as well.

The *Washington Post* reported that "While many Americans search in vain for flu shots, members and employees of Congress are able to obtain them quickly and at no charge from the Capitol's attending physician, who has urged all 535 lawmakers to get the vaccines even if they are young and healthy."

A spokesperson for the congressional physician, Dr. John F. Eisold, said that "people of all ages who are credentialed to work in the Capitol can get a shot by saying they meet the guidelines, with no further questions asked."

The policy applied to thousands of legislative staffers, police officers, construction workers, restaurant employees, journalists, and others who work in the Capitol complex. Those most directly and specifically encouraged to violate the CDC guidelines, though, were senators and congresspeople.

Senate Majority Leader Bill Frist (R-Tenn), a heart surgeon, sent letters urging his 99 colleagues to get the shots because they mingle and shake hands with so many people.

Eisold, too, used the hand-shaking argument to urge all 535 lawmakers to get shots.

The entire process of vaccination in the United States, Caplan said in a telephone interview, is "ethically bizarre. You have the most effective intervention in medicine hanging by a thread. Everyone's crying out for evidence-based medicine—well, there's no better evidence-based medicine than vaccination."

And when vaccines are in short supply, flu shots become like exit visas from a war zone, and ethical problems arise that amount to what he called "a complete moral breakdown."

"We don't have anybody in clear authority to control the supply of vaccine. Because individual health organizations make individual contracts with the suppliers, the person making the decision who gets it and who doesn't might be the director of a student health organization, the governor of a state, the director of a VA hospital, the head of a clinic. Nobody's in charge. Consequently, one group of the public may be hearing that they can't get a shot while across the street anyone can be vaccinated, high-risk or not."

Seeing this set of contradictions all too clearly, New Jersey Senator Joseph Vitale (D-Middlesex) proposed a bill that would levy a $500 fine for doctors, pharmacists, and other medical professionals who vaccinate a low-

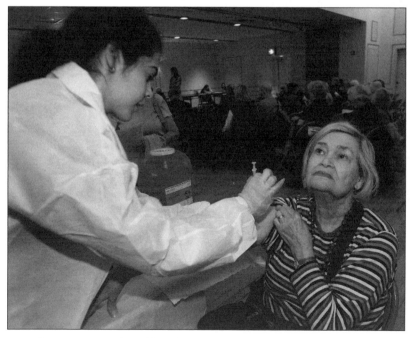

New York Department of Health technician Sarah Pollak (L) administers a flu shot to Barbara Sacks at the YWCA in New York City, November 17, 2004. (*Photograph by Don Emmert/AFP/Getty Images*)

risk person, and additional penalties for repeat offenders. The bill also gave state health officials the power to redirect any available vaccine to vulnerable residents—children under 22 months, adults over 64, people with chronic medical conditions, pregnant women, nursing home residents, and those, particularly health care workers, who have contact with high-risk people. Other bills required the state to contract with pharmaceutical companies to purchase influenza vaccine for high-risk persons and their care providers, provided immunity for the DHHS and local health departments that distribute or administer influenza vaccine, required state purchase and distribution of influenza vaccine, and required the Commissioner of DHHS to annually determine the amount of influenza vaccine needed for a State and obtain that vaccine.

Yet Caplan's paradox remained:Who would regulate such laws? Who would enforce them?

Any set of guidelines would have to take into consideration that the priorities would change under differing circumstances. The SARS epidemic, for example, showed how quickly a country could be brought to its knees if the first to fall sick were the healthcare workers.

"During a pandemic, everything changes," pointed out Dr. Alan Hinman, former longtime director of immunization and prevention services at the CDC. The likelihood of any country having a stockpile of the right vaccine, a stockpile large enough for the entire population, is probably zero. Shortages are inevitable. "So should physicians, nurses, ambulance workers and hospital staff be vaccinated first? Should those at highest risk of death from influenza (our usual target group) be vaccinated first? Or should the first priority be to make sure that society keeps moving on a bedrock level, in which case the first to be vaccinated might be police officers and firefighters?"

Any broad-scale emergency vaccination program would have to be flexible enough to designate different priorities for different epidemics—and the public would have to accept that.

| The Canadian Dimension

As if these complications at home weren't enough, the crisis immediately took on international dimensions.

In a televised debate, President Bush suggested Canada might help the U.S., but this suggestion seemed more like a gambit than a solution. Health Canada said perhaps another 500,000 to 1 million doses might be excess that could be retrieved from clinics and made available to the United States, but even so, Canada's vaccines were not approved for use in the United States—a point Bush was making on other occasions in proposing legislation to ban the import of cheaper prescription drugs from Canada.

"There is massive hypocrisy on the part of the Bush administration," said Jillian Claire Cohen, an assistant professor of pharmacy at the University of Toronto. "They are very hesitant to allow cheaper, safe drugs from Canada, but when it serves their purposes, all of a sudden they turn to Canada."

Canada's largest vaccine producer, ID Biomedical, contacted the Food and Drug Administration to say that it could spare 1.2 million doses. But with the U.S. shortfall estimated at 40 million doses, it was a little more than a gesture—and a cynical one, perhaps. A spokeswoman for ID Biomedical acknowledged to Canadian reporters that the company was starting a large expansion and had planned to seek FDA approval of its vaccine by 2007.

Sure enough, a few weeks later ID Biomedical changed its position and said it would not be selling vaccine to the U.S.

"The reality of the matter is there is a need in Canada," said Dr. Tony Holler, ID Biomedical's chief executive officer, according to the Canadian Press agency in Montreal. Several Canadian newspapers reported that Holler said once it became apparent selling the surplus to the U.S. would not aid the company in its efforts to get accelerated licensing approval in that market, the decision was made to sell to Canadian purchasers. "We were not going to gain any advantage from this," Holler said.

If U.S.-Canadian cooperation was not going to happen on a national scale, though, this didn't stop people taking the neighborly relationship into their own hands.

When Americans began driving across the border into Canada to get flu shots, Ontario Health Ministry officials held a conference call with the province's 37 public health officers and instructed them to start demanding proof of Ontario residency before giving anyone the vaccine.

The ruling applied only to public health facilities, though, and Urgent Care Niagara, a private company with small clinics in Niagara Falls and Fort Erie, made the vaccine available to high-risk U.S. residents at $50 Canadian a shot. It was inundated with calls after a Buffalo radio station gave out its number during morning rush hour, resulting in some lines at the Fort Erie clinic, said Dr. Artaj Singh, the company's medical director.

A "Flu Bus" was chartered to run from Grand Forks, North Dakota to Winnipeg, Canada, for $99 round-trip, with lunch at Olive Garden or Red Lobster and a flu shot thrown in. A Vancouver clinic network, Vancouver Coastal Health, gave shots to several hundred Americans who made the three-hour drive from Seattle.

Perhaps the most novel operation was a 330-passenger "flu cruise" ferry that ran from Seattle, Washington, to Victoria, British Columbia. For $105, passengers got a round-trip ticket and a flu shot on the dockside in Victoria. Some days, patients determined to get their shots braved 6- to 8-foot seas and 40-knot winds in the Strait of Juan de Fuca.

Joshua Tewell, 28, who made the journey with his son, Austin, 2, said he had made five attempts to get a flu shot near his home in Woodinville, Washington. His wife had just given birth to their second son ten weeks prematurely, and Mr. Tewell said he would not be allowed to visit the baby in intensive care without being immunized.

"Any kind of disease is life-threatening to him," Mr. Tewell said. He got off the boat, went through customs, lined up with the others, and then held his crying son tightly as a nurse gave the boy the injection.

Pressure may have been applied behind the scenes, though, for on October 29, 2004, it was reported that after a little more than a week in service, the ferry was finished.

The Canadian clinic that had been providing the vaccine could no longer guarantee a supply, said Darrell Bryan, executive vice-president of Clipper Navigation.

"Clipper understands and respects that Canada's first priority for allocation of the flu vaccine is to its own citizens," Bryan said piously to the *Vancouver Sun*. "Although we are pleased to have been able to help many American senior citizens and other high-risk people, without a guaranteed supply of vaccine available . . . it would be irresponsible for us to continue to sell the flu shots."

In the end, these activities turned out to be no more than border skirmishes, yet they highlight a problem that, in the case of a pandemic, would be overwhelming.

"The ethical implications are global," said D.A. Henderson. The same lack of any clear policy for the regulation and distribution of vaccine within the U.S. would play out on a planetary scale, and with much higher stakes. "Even if, in the case of a pandemic, the U.S. manages to scrape together 150 million doses, who should get them? It's not just a question of who in the U.S. should get them. It will be a global epidemic, after all—so what if the areas worst affected are in, say, China and Africa? Is the U.S. going to sit on its vaccine supply when 10% of the world is dying? The political implications are horrifying—yet so is the alternative. You can imagine the attitude in the U.S. if some of the vaccine gets sent to China."

| Some Vagaries of Funding

A nother crucial detail in the flu vaccine picture was that while most vaccines are routinely given to virtually all children, flu vaccine is recommended on a voluntary basis and is not strictly a childhood vaccine.

These two differences produced an entirely different landscape of vaccination.

First, most vaccines can be ordered with at least a certain sense of how many doses will be needed; flu vaccine usage tends to vary widely based on factors including the public's perception of risk and other factors. The likelihood of either shortage or waste, then, is much greater.

Second, the routine nature of childhood vaccinations means that an infrastructure already exists to carry out vaccinations: motive, means, and opportunity are well established. But vaccinating adults is a far more ad hoc business. If a flu pandemic struck, where would vaccinations take place? When? Who would contact the adult, and how? Who would keep records? And—a callous question, but an unavoidable one—how much profit would be legitimate?

Which brings us to the third difference: funding. For four decades, the United States has had a broad childhood immunization program. In 1962, Section 317 of the Public Health Service Act set aside money to buy vaccine for children and to set up the infrastructure necessary to get the vaccine to the kids. In 1993, the Vaccines for Children (VFC) Program made childhood immunizations an entitlement: any child who is on Medicaid or is a Native American or Alaska Native is entitled to be vaccinated through this program. In addition, children are eligible for VFC if they are under-insured with respect to vaccination and receive their vaccines at a Federally Qualified Health Center or Rural Health Clinic. As a result, children have something of a safety net. Adults have no such net.

| A Public Health Nightmare

By the end of October, shortages were being reported everywhere around the United States.

In Vermont, after state officials said that the state was short 50,000 doses of flu vaccine, the Roman Catholic Diocese of Burlington formally asked its more than 100 priests to refrain from using the communion chalice and suggested its 148,000 parishioners avoid the usual handshake, hug, or kiss when they make the sign of peace during Mass until the end of flu season. The ban went into effect on October 31 and was to run until Easter Sunday, March 27, 2005.

Several counties in Maryland started holding or planning second-generation lotteries—in other words, lotteries for any vaccine that had not been used up by nursing home patients and other people with high priority. Even these leftover doses would still be assigned only to young children, the elderly, and others at high risk if they catch the flu—and lucky enough to get a winning number. In Montgomery County, 20,630 people applied for the lottery of 800 available doses.

A new form of drive-through was invented: the drive-through flu vaccination center, an alternative to the public relations nightmare of hundreds of elderly people lining up in the cold for hours on end. Newspapers reported that thousands of people, some driving for hours, had stampeded the drive-throughs, including one in Magnolia, Arkansas, where the lucky few could stick their arms out their car windows and be vaccinated.

"It's a nightmare," said Christine Mahon, a nurse at the Maricopa County Department of Public Health in Arizona, one of many health agencies across the country that were flooded with calls and visits by people seeking shots that were often not available. "This is a very hard place to work right now."

The public were beginning to get their flu shots, but this wasn't a sign that the system was working. Far from it—it was a sign that public health authorities were trying to make up for the lack of a broad-based vaccination infrastructure by taking the task on themselves—a task for which they were pitifully underequipped, understaffed, and underfunded.

Public health was being stressed at every level. On a national level, the CDC's National Immunization Program, struggling to coordinate the efforts of dozens of different players, was massively overextended. "We were swamped," said Dr. Stephen Cochi, the program's acting director. "It was a huge redirection of attention and effort."

The crisis highlighted another way in which flu vaccination differs from other vaccinations. Most vaccination programs are run by public health agencies, but under normal circumstances only about 10–15% of flu vaccines are bought by public health. The vast majority, 85–90%, are bought on a market-based system by private groups. "That system basically ground to a halt," Cochi explained. "Everything reverted to the expectation that public health officials would clean up the mess."

A health official in New York said, "If you were a private doctor, there was no way for you to get vaccine. All we could do was provide information and, really, triage."

It also meant that there was no well-developed infrastructure for vaccinating adults—an issue that is bound to arise in spades in the event of a pandemic.

The same systemic overload happened at the municipal and state levels.

"We came within hours of having to close our health clinics," Dr. Thomas R. Frieden, commissioner of New York City's Department of Health and Mental Hygiene, told the *New York Times*. Only a last-minute donation of 10,000 doses from Beth Israel Medical Center kept the clinics running.

In nine weeks city health workers vaccinated more than 55,000 people, compared to 20,000 in the same period a year previously. In October alone, the department took 71,000 calls about vaccinations. According to the *New York Times*, the city "scrounged" 23,000 doses from Oklahoma and 44,000 more from suppliers of federal institutions such as veterans' hospitals. The city was partly able to survive by using one of the procedures that had been designed and implemented since the anthrax attacks of October 2001—taking over city buses to move people to and from temporary clinics, for example.

Virginia was no less overstressed than New York. Testifying before Congress, Dr. Robert Stroube, state health commissioner of Virginia, explained how the crisis was playing out in his state. The piecemeal, market-based system of buying and distributing vaccine had broken down, and the task of dealing with the crisis had been left, willy-nilly, to the state. "You might say that the health department is now the 'broker' in the management of the flu vaccine to help ensure that the vaccine goes where it is most needed."

The state wasn't in a position to establish or monitor consistency in distribution, though, Stroube explained, so each health district had "developed a flu vaccine distribution plan based on the needs of the high-risk persons in that community.... In some areas, they opened up the phone lines and began taking appointments on a first call-first served basis, some distributed the vaccine to other health care providers in the community, some pre-identified high-risk individuals who are unable to get the vaccine in the private sector."

Virginia was one state that had tried the "drive-through" method, but it placed an appalling burden on public health staff. According to Stroube, one clinic alone, in Chesterfield County, just outside of Richmond, "required 120 staff members to manage all of the logistics. The health director there estimates that this ongoing issue has required more than 600 hours of work from senior-level managers, supervisors and other personnel. The health department's time devoted to this ongoing flu shortage supply issue means time away from other important public health practices."

And what about nursing homes and long-term care facilities, arguably the population at highest risk, that had contracted to buy their vaccine from

Chiron? The state health department had managed to acquire some 82,000 doses of vaccine, but now all 35 health districts in Virginia had to interview and survey every facility in their communities to assess how much was needed, where, and how soon.

It was like the SARS epidemic in Toronto: virtually everyone employed by public health had to drop their usual jobs and throw themselves into the crisis. "In our immunization program," Stroube said, "we typically only need one full time person working on the flu vaccine program. This year, we have four staff persons working continuously managing this issue at the state level. In addition, the issue has required the involvement of all of our senior-level management, our public information personnel and some of our emergency preparedness personnel, who manage state level planning, logistics, communication and coordination."

Even with all of the flu vaccine that was now coming into Virginia, Stroube testified, "we do not expect that we will have enough vaccine for every high-risk individual in Virginia this year." Instead, the state was trying to limit the spread of disease by recommending bedrock public health practices: hand washing, staying home from work when sick. It was the lessons of SARS all over again.

| America Isolated

In November and early December, the FDA's "gold standard" approach took a further pounding as states and the federal government began negotiations to import vaccine from Germany and Britain.

Health and Human Services Secretary Tommy Thompson said the government was immediately buying 1.2 million doses of the vaccine, called Fluarix, which was available immediately, and said British manufacturer, GlaxoSmithKline, had agreed to make about 3 million more doses available at a later date.

The German-made vaccine, Fluarix, had not been licensed for use in the United States, so it would be available as an "investigational new drug," meaning that it could be used but patients would have to sign a consent form acknowledging there could be risks. Patients receiving the "experimental" vaccine might also have to pay an additional fee of $18–$25.

The FDA announced that its inspectors had signed off on the vaccine's safety after inspecting the facilities where it was made. The officials also tested to be sure that the vaccines would be effective against the dominant flu strain expected in the United States and made sure it had been stored properly since it had been made.

Yet a CDC survey showed that, in terms of public opinion, the damage had already been done. When adults at high risk were asked if they would be willing to take the vaccine after being told that it was "investigational," only 56% said yes, and then only if no other vaccine were available. When asked if they would take the vaccine knowing that they would be required to sign the FDA waiver, willingness dropped to 40%.

Separately, Illinois, New Mexico, and New York City reported that their health authorities had located another 650,000 doses from drug wholesalers in Europe and were trying to buy doses in this fashion, but the *New York Times* reported in January that "Health officials said that it was difficult to determine the safety of the vaccine from overseas quickly and that the Food and Drug Administration therefore stopped the deal."

An international accord on drug safety standards was clearly still a long way off.

| More Vagaries of Funding

Buying vaccines from abroad raised another controversy: how to pay for them? Public health was having to pick up the tab for medical care that would normally be funneled through private providers.

After the initial relief that another source of vaccine had been found, the news emerged that the federal government was buying these doses of "experimental" vaccines by diverting funds that had been earmarked for vaccinating low-income children.

To pay for these vaccines, it was reported, the government would dip into a $220 million grant program intended to help provide routine vaccinations to children of families who were too poor to be fully insured, but who are not poor enough to be eligible under state Medicaid programs. Money for such vaccinations was already so scarce that nineteen states were struggling with their vaccination programs.

One of those states was Nebraska, whose chief medical officer, Dr. Richard Raymond, said that if the federal government cut financing for the children's vaccine program to pay for experimental flu vaccines, his state might vaccinate fewer children. Under the government's plan, money would be deducted from childhood immunization programs to pay for the experimental flu vaccine even in states that did not receive the experimental doses.

"We should not be pitting vaccines for children against vaccines for adults," said Mary Selecky, the secretary of health in Washington State.

| Vaccine Shortages and the Prospect of Pandemic Influenza

When Tommy G. Thompson resigned as Health and Human Services Secretary on December 3, 2004, he said that what worried him most was the threat of an avian flu pandemic. "This is a really huge bomb that could adversely impact on the health care of the world," killing 30 million to 70 million people, he said.

Five days later, a WHO release underscored Thompson's words. "Even in the best case scenarios of the next pandemic, two to seven million people would die and tens of millions would require medical attention," the WHO announced. "If the next pandemic virus is a very virulent strain, deaths could be dramatically higher.

"The global spread of a pandemic cannot be stopped but preparedness will reduce its impact. WHO will continue to urge preparedness and assist Member States in these activities. In the next few weeks, WHO will be publishing a national assessment tool to evaluate and focus national preparedness efforts. WHO will also be providing guidance on stockpiling antivirals and vaccines. Next week, WHO will be convening an expert meeting on preparedness planning. WHO is also working to advance development of pandemic virus vaccines, and to expedite research efforts to understand the mechanisms of emergence and spread of influenza pandemics.

71

"It is of central importance that Member States take the necessary steps to develop their own preparedness plans. Some have already developed structures and processes to counter this threat but some plans are far from complete and many Member States have yet to begin.

"WHO believes the appearance of H5N1, which is now widely entrenched in Asia, signals that the world has moved closer to the next pandemic. While it is impossible to accurately forecast the magnitude of the next pandemic, we do know that much of the world is unprepared for a pandemic of any size."

Yet the WHO warning went largely unreported in the United States. Despite the Chiron fallout, the flu vaccine shortage and the avian flu epidemic seemed literally a world apart. To the U.S., the avian flu was an Asian phenomenon; to the rest of the world, the flu vaccine shortage was an American problem.

If the history of flu has proven anything over and over again, it's that flu (and infectious disease in general) is a global problem.

Dr. Alan Hinman understands the situation better than most. He worked for ten years as director of the immunization division at the CDC, and another seven years as director of prevention services at the CDC, which included immunizations. He takes the likelihood of pandemic flu very seriously, he said.

"A colleague of mine says, 'The pandemic clock is ticking—we just don't know what time it is.'"

In a normal year, the target population for flu vaccination is about 185 million, "of whom we regularly reach half, or fewer." Even the at-risk elderly are still only vaccinated at a rate of about 60–70%.

In a pandemic, the United States would need some 600 million doses of vaccine, given that two doses would likely be needed for each person.

The 2004 vaccine shortage showed how hard it is, under current conditions, to guarantee even 100 million doses, let alone 300 million, and how hard it is to make up a shortfall of a mere 50 million doses. During a pandemic the country would be trying to triple the number of doses—a task that would, in Hinman's words, severely strain a production system even with all its suppliers working at full capacity. Worst of all, the frantic scramble of October and November 2004 has shown how hard it is to deliver whatever vaccine is available to those who most need it. The situation has been a warning shot; it remains to be seen whether it will be heard around the world.

| Too Much Vaccine

As December progressed and the flu season proper began, a peculiar change came over the U.S.: all of a sudden there seemed to be too much vaccine. Four-fifths of states said they had enough or more than enough vaccine. The Tennessee Department of Health announced in mid-December that 48,000 doses of the flu vaccine would be distributed to the state's 95 counties. Tennessee health departments said they had received over 60% more vaccines than last year. Officials in California, Colorado, and Washington announced that they had vaccinated all the high-risk patients who had come along for a shot and still had thousands of doses left over.

"Many of us are now concerned we will not use vaccine supplies. The only sin this season is to leave vaccine on the shelf," said Dr. William Schaffner, an influenza vaccine expert and head of preventive medicine at Vanderbilt University Medical Center in Nashville.

A combination of events had turned the situation on its head. First, the frantic reallocation of vaccine had met its goal, and in most areas of the country, most high-risk patients had been able to get a shot. At the same time, reported the CDC, many high-risk patients had apparently given up on being able to get vaccinated, and had just not bothered to seek out a shot. Third, a strange kind of law of crisis supply and demand had apparently gone into effect: while shots seemed scarce, people were desperate to be vaccinated, but as soon as the scarcity seemed to be over, it no longer seemed as important to get a shot. And the flu season started late and mild, so the urgency seemed even less. Rather than letting vaccine go to waste, individual states began lowering the bar and offering vaccinations to everyone over 50.

The *New York Times* reported that as soon as the city had sufficient vaccine, demand began to drop off. Flu hotlines were actually receiving fewer calls than at the same time last year. Ironically, flu vaccinations were slumping just as the flu season began, with about 1,000 people a day turning up at hospitals with flu-like symptoms, and 40 outbreaks reported at nursing homes.

It wasn't as if everyone who needed a shot had received one. The CDC's *Morbidity and Mortality Weekly Report* published the results of two surveys suggesting that many adults in priority groups had been unable to get vaccinated.

According to one survey, "Among adults in priority groups who had not yet received influenza vaccine, 23.3% reported that they attempted to obtain vaccination but could not; among persons aged >65 years, the proportion was 32.5%.... Among adults not in a priority group who had not received vaccine, 10.4% reported that they attempted to obtain vaccination but could not. Among adults in priority groups, 10.0% of adults said they were saving the vaccine for others, and 6.5% thought that they were not eligible to receive the vaccine."

A second survey analyzed the results slightly differently, concluding that "approximately 63% of persons aged >65 years and 46% of chronically ill adults who tried to get the influenza vaccine were able to do so. More than half of adults at high risk did not try to get the influenza vaccine."

As 2004 drew to a close, the flu vaccine shortage came to what was arguably one of the worse possible outcomes: an anticlimax. The very real possibility was that the entire situation would seem to be a cry of "Wolf!" Elected officials and the public might relegate the double issue of vaccines and influenza to an even lower shelf in the file cabinet of their attention.

Above all, explained Dick Raymond of ASTHO, the whole concept of routine vaccination, a concept that public health officials work very hard and long to instill into members of the public, has been shaken.

"Some people in the 50–64 age range who didn't get their vaccination will be mad at us, especially if they subsequently got the flu. Then they'll be really ticked at us because we wouldn't let them have [the vaccine]." Conversely, he added, "some people who reluctantly get a shot every year may now be looking around at a relatively mild flu season and thinking that flu vaccination isn't that important after all, causing us to lose ground in our effort to reduce influenza morbidity and mortality."

From the makers' point of view, this is yet another blow to the likelihood of steady, predictable and preferably growing demand—which according to Chris Grant, is "as important, even more important, than buying demand with government dollars."

Vaccination Coverage Among Adults

"...influenza vaccination coverage among healthy persons aged 18-64 years who were not health-care workers or contacts of children aged <6 months was lower than in the previous season (8.8% compared with 17.8%)" (*CDC, unpublished data, 2005*). Among the reasons cited by respondents for not receiving vaccination, was "saving vaccine for people who need it more," cited by 9.3% of those who were not in priority groups and were not vaccinated. This represents approximately 17.5 million doses of vaccine potentially made available to persons in priority groups.

—*April 1, 2005 issue of Morbidity and Mortality Weekly Report (MMWR)*

| Less Than Obvious Lessons

"**T**he lesson for the future seems obvious," editorialized the *New York Times*, which called the Chiron affair a "fiasco." "A stronger, faster-acting, more flexible manufacturing base for influenza vaccine is badly needed. Officials called yesterday for cell-culture technologies that could expand capacity or shift direction quickly in making flu vaccines, as well as for the greater availability of eggs to make vaccines the traditional way. Other experts have suggested that governments should buy a lot more vaccine in normal years, a move that could yield immediate health benefits while enticing more manufacturers to enter the field. If there is a silver lining in this crisis, it may be the recognition that our whole approach to making flu vaccines must be modernized."

Actually, the lessons are not that obvious, and as the United States moved through the heart of the 2004–2005 flu season, the outcomes of the Chiron "fiasco" were even less obvious. It wasn't at all clear how to develop a "stronger, faster-acting, more flexible manufacturing base."

Drug companies, for example, used the vaccine shortage as a bargaining chip. At recent congressional hearings, MedImmune argued two ways to avoid shortages in future. One was for the CDC to recommend that everyone (or at least all school-age children, their parents, and grandparents) be routinely vaccinated against flu, which would expand demand for vaccines and thus improve their profitability. The other was for the government to give tax incentives for research and development, especially the development of cell-based vaccine manufacturing, and for construction of U.S.-based facilities. At the same hearings Chiron, which would hardly seem to be in a position to demand lower standards of regulation, argued for what its CEO called a "regulatory pathway that fosters innovation." He also called for mechanisms to reasonably protect vaccine manufacturers from liability claims, even though liability claims have never been a major issue in flu vaccine manufacture.

At the same hearings, Representative John Tierney (D-Mass) pointed out that these recommendations amounted to a one-way street. If the government offers tax breaks, he said, "That is making the taxpayer an investor. It's no longer a free market. If you want the taxpayer to be an investor, what is the return? Royalties? A share of the profits? Price controls? A guaranteed supply?"

Certainly, protecting the interests of the drug companies as a way of wooing them back to the U.S. is a far cry from Ontario's free-flu-shots-for-all commitment.

Other informed observers, such as Dr. Michael Osterholm, Director of the Center for Infectious Disease Research & Policy at the University of Minnesota, suggest that both the welfare state model and the free market model are outdated, and a new model is needed.

"We need to have a fundamental change in this country and around the world," he said. "We've got to figure out a relationship that motivates pharmaceutical companies to make vaccine a priority." He suggested ("as repugnant as this whole approach may seem to some in the public health community") a procurement model like the one used by the Department of Defense to buy military equipment. "It's not a free market model—without the Department of Defense as a buyer, the arms companies wouldn't exist—but it offers the manufacturers a very specialized and vastly rewarding niche.... They build a vaccine and we'll buy it."

The danger with such a model, of course, is that it is notoriously prone to overcharging and corruption.

Under one initiative, Congress has indeed funded a huge increase in funding for research and development of vaccines. Project BioShield, an initiative of the Bush White House that was signed into law on July 21, 2004, provided $5.6 billion over ten years to improve medical countermeasures protecting Americans against a chemical, biological, radiological, or nuclear attack. These measures are to include 75 million doses of a second-generation anthrax vaccine, botulinum antitoxin, and smallpox vaccine. This expensive program, though, has little to do with flu—or, in fact, most other plausible epidemics.

"They're creating a very expensive program against diseases that don't exist anywhere in the world," said Dr. William Schaffner. "What we need is an adult immunization program for diseases that kill tens of thousands every year."

In the short term, the easiest way to make more vaccine available to the American public may be by creating universal manufacturing standards, and streamlining what D.A. Henderson called "a very cumbersome FDA licensing procedure," enabling the U.S. to buy vaccine from as many different makers as, say, European governments. If this happens, and if GlaxoSmithKline and ID Biomedical choose to enter the American market, the entire debate takes a different tack.

The *Times'* call for cell-culture manufacturing may reflect an all too familiar American belief that the answer to social problems lies in better technology. Even Aventis' Jim Matthews, who is committed to developing new manufacturing methods, admits that Aventis has been trying to make cell-culture technology work for as long as he has been at the company— more than ten years—and it may be another ten years before it is finally practicable, if at all.

The "greater availability of eggs" has been addressed already, and can be seen as one practical outcome of the vaccine shortage. The federal government has intervened to shore up Aventis' egg-based production by offering one contract that enables the plant to operate year-round instead of on a nine-month basis, and another contract to allow Aventis to foster backup flocks in different areas of the country so production would be less vulnerable to, say, an avian flu epidemic that swept through its chicken farms.

As for "buying more vaccine in normal years," a number of states are already considering or have passed legislation to enable the state health department to buy sufficient vaccine for the coming season, which might well "yield immediate health benefits while enticing more manufacturers to enter the field." But this is still at best a patchwork system, it has yet to pass the rigorous test of annual budget hearings, and Americans are not accustomed to appropriating such sums for public health initiatives. Along similar lines, the National Vaccine Advisory Committee is recommending that the nation develop an adult influenza immunization program, one that makes vaccine available free of charge to adolescents and adults, provides for Medicare reimbursement, and also sets up the organization necessary to do the job, but if the current flu season turns out to be a mild one, such good intentions may be indefinitely postponed.

Yet the *Times'* recommendations, like the U.S. pandemic influenza plan, fail to address two areas of paramount importance.

One is the interlocking questions of ethics and infrastructure. There are still no clear, broad-scale guidelines for who should be vaccinated first, in case of an epidemic or pandemic, and how the massive effort of that vaccination should be organized or funded. It bears repeating: flu vaccine cannot be stockpiled. At the beginning of a pandemic, there will be shortages, probably for months rather than weeks. Changes in vaccine production won't affect that situation one iota. The usual means of buying, distributing, and administering vaccine will collapse. The ethical nightmare of deciding who gets vaccine first won't have been resolved, and the whole mess will be thrown into the lap of an underfunded and understaffed public health system once more.

Alan Hinman said that the NVAC is trying to marshall public input with a view to making policy recommendations by June 2005, and a new CDC ethics panel may well be considering this question, but these groups have not yet reached the discussion stage.

The other area that needs to be considered is as vast as the planet. Especially in the U.S., influenza planning tends to think along national lines rather than in terms of the world as a whole, where in the case of a pandemic the problems will be the same, but on a much larger, global scale. Without a universal set of production standards and sufficient production capacity, vaccine shortages will run into billions, not millions.

And who will decide who gets the available vaccine, and whether vaccine should be sent to Haiti or Somalia?

It would be an avoidable tragedy if the flu vaccine shortage had the effect of making the U.S. think ever more provincially, of circling the wagons and creating the illusion of homeland security in the face of infectious disease.

| No Bioshield

Ironically, just as the flu vaccine shortage began to ease late in 2004, new information emerged about a familiar danger: the Spanish Flu pandemic of 1918–1919.

In research by epidemiologists Christina Mills and Marc Lipsitch of the Harvard School of Public Health, published in the journal *Nature*, the Harvard team studied the spread of Spanish flu in 45 U.S. cities and discovered that on average only two to four people were infected for every person that caught the virus. By contrast, the rate of infection per case for measles in an unvaccinated population would be as high as 17 people. In other words, Spanish flu might have been deadly, but it wasn't especially contagious.

Mills and Lipsitch claimed their research showed that a targeted program of vaccines and antiviral drugs could halt a pandemic, providing medical authorities had the resources to act swiftly and decisively.

"Before this study, estimates were all over the map on the transmissibility of pandemic flu," said Lipsitch, associate professor of epidemiology at Harvard.

"Some thought it was so transmissible that vaccines would be unlikely to stop it. This study is optimistic, except we don't have the vaccine.

"It is now even more important to put resources into the development of vaccine technology, manufacture and distribution systems to make possible a rapid response to the next outbreak of an entirely new flu strain. We need to have our manufacturing system functional quickly."

"What's happening with the flu vaccine shortage are lessons that we need to think more globally," said Dr. Stephen Cochi. "We're all in this together, and the goal is to have a sufficient, stable vaccine supply to lessen the blow of an unpredicted event.... There's been a lot of talk about this, but too little action."

Osterholm agreed. The United States, he said, can't afford to think in isolationist terms. "We need to protect the world, and in so doing protect ourselves."

There isn't much of a precedent for this kind of global initiative, he said. In the case of HIV/AIDS, for example, there have been some public health successes but "some worldwide dropping of the ball." If the world as a whole can't work together to deal with a pandemic that is already in motion, he said, how will it cooperate in the development and distribution of vaccines?

The world has no bioshield, and in the event of a pandemic, everyone will pay one way or another.

| Resources for More Information

American Public Health Association: **www.apha.org**

Centers for Disease Control and Prevention: **www.cdc.gov/flu/**

World Health Organization: **www.who.int/csr/disease/influenza/en/**